UNLEASHED

DIARY OF A WOMAN VET

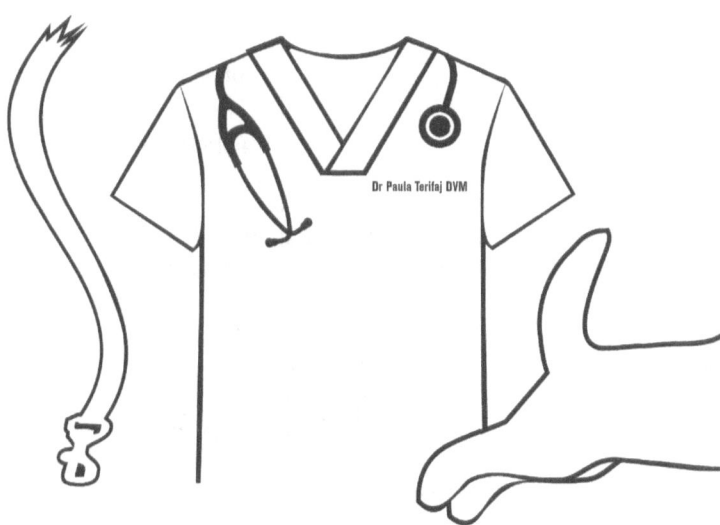

Dr Paula Terifaj DVM

Copyright © 2019 by Dr Paula Terifaj DVM

All rights exclusively reserved. No part of this book may be reproduced or translated into any language or utilized in any form or by any means, electronic or mechanical, including photocopying, recording or by any information storage and retrieval system, without permission in writing from the publisher.

Terifaj, Paula
Unleashed, Diary of a Woman Vet

First Edition
Library of Congress Control Number:2019909742

ISBN 978-0-578-52450-4 (paperback)

Published by
Dr Paula Terifaj DVM
Desert Hot Springs, California

Interior Design & Layout
Mark E. Anderson

www.aquazebra.com

Printed in the United States of America

Dedication

Nothing has warmed my heart more than my ability to assist the rescue community. As a witness to sometimes heroic efforts, there is nothing more satisfying than to see helpless and sometimes neglected pets find protection and compassion in your loving hands. Your dedication to these have-nots is a noble calling.

It is my greatest desire that the stories I tell will create a greater awareness for the many sacrifices made to thwart the cruelty of an outdated shelter system. To all those that volunteer and donate resources – giving unwanted pets a second chance - you remain my heroes!

Table of Contents

Part 1: Vet School 1
Chapter 1: Woman Vet 3
Chapter 2: Mailbox 9
Chapter 3: Vet School 15
Chapter 4: Petey 21
Chapter 5: Home, Sweet Home.. 25
Part 2: Career..31
Chapter 6: Death and the Curiosity that Saved Cats 33
Chapter 7: Survival.. 39
Chapter 8: Lucky Charm 45
Chapter 9: Denver... 49
Chapter 10: Lucy...59
Chapter 11: Rose 65
Chapter 12: Woody... 69
Chapter 13: People Food...73
Chapter 14: The Dogie Bag 77
Chapter 15: Lola.. 83
Chapter 16: Brad Pit 93
Part 3: New Beginnings 97
Chapter 17: Going Broke 99
Chapter 18: Sabbatical...105
Chapter 19: The Bet 109
Chapter 20: Reboot..113
Chapter 21: Save A Pet 117
Chapter 22: Breaking News... 123

Chapter 23: Opportunity Knocks 127
Chapter 24: Ace in the Hole 133
Chapter 25: Joe's Plan 143
Chapter 26: Date with Destiny 147
Chapter 27: Flower 151
Chapter 28: First Call 155
Epilogue 159
About the Author 163
Appendix 165

Part One

Vet School

Chapter One

Woman Vet

Security is mostly a superstition. Life is either a daring adventure or nothing.
—Helen Keller

I first overheard someone call me the "woman vet" sometime after I built and opened my own veterinary hospital in 1988. My acceptance into veterinary school was a first—for women, that is. The year was 1982 and it marked the first time that women equaled the number of men accepted; it was a tie. Some referred to us as the 50/50 class. That was the first time I pondered the significance of being a woman in a previously male-dominated field. Four years later, when I graduated—an accomplishment in and of itself—being female seemed to really matter for the first time in my life. I realized that while I personally had nothing to prove by my gender, society did. I took it as a compliment, nonetheless. But that fact turned out to be more of an advantage. I was the first and only female doctor in town. People actually liked that.

If you are reading this book, it's because I had to overcome some big hurdles after thinking about writing something like this for years. In fact, all I had was part of this title, *A Woman Vet*...a title without a single word on paper. I never told anyone about it because it just seemed too big. The task was just too daunting. I even doubted that I had the guts and determination to birth a book. So, as I write this sentence, I am trusting that I do have something to say and that it will matter to someone and that I will stick it out. Also, because I am going to be completely honest, I've had a lot of extra time on my hands since I retired from practice. I'm a little bored. And today was especially boring. So here we go.

I was not that kid who was supposed to go to college. In high school, I was more interested in boys and riding horses. To keep my parents, Paul and Virginia, satisfied, I could not fall below a C average. I had a firm C-plus keeping me out of trouble. My top priorities at age seventeen were to keep playing with boys, get a job so I could afford to move out of the family home, get my own place, and do my own thing—whatever that was. By the time I was twenty-three, I was lost. I hated the job, broke up with my cheating boyfriend, and gained some unwanted weight. I was somewhat depressed, and life seemed dull.

Months later a well-meaning friend, who knew I was an animal lover, dropped off a book one day in an attempt to cheer me up. It looked like one of those silly little animal books, so it sat around for weeks on the coffee table. The voice inside my head told me that I was not one of those silly pet-lover types. I was too serious for that fluffy stuff. Until one day, while stuck at home and feeling bored (there is that bored thing again), I picked up the paperback, *All Creatures Great and Small*, written under the pseudonym James Herriot. The real hero in the stories was British veterinary surgeon Alf Wight. This collection of short stories, inspired by Wight's years of devotion making friends and house calls along the bumpy roadside of Yorkshire Dales, England, spoke to me. In fact, it spoke volumes, like an edict. When I discovered his new sequel, *All Things Wise and Wonderful* had just been published, I rushed to read it. I'll never know just when it happened—which book or which page I was reading—but it happened. Alf had become my mentor and I, the most eager student he could have ever had. The C-student with lousy high school SAT exam scores was going to college—a two-year community college. So they had to let me in.

If I could time-travel back to my college days, I'd go back to thank the humble college counselor who was assigned to me. I had boldly declared my full-fledged intent to become a pre-veterinary student and he had the unpleasant task of reviewing my entrance exam scores. I would thank him for what he *did not* do. He did not discourage me in any way or make me feel like I could not cut the mustard. I'm sure others would have suggested an alternative path—like what happened to my sister, Sandra. My sister was working in a dress shop and had an eye for fashion. During her college interview (we attended the same community college), she expressed her desire to enter the field of psychology. After her review with her counselor, she was put on the fast track for the fashion design industry. Several unhappy years later, she went back to college for a do-over in psychology. Ultimately, she became a beautifully well-dressed marriage and family counselor—and loved it. So what did my wise and gray-haired counselor do? He signed me up for two bonehead classes: remedial English and math. If you failed to get the significance of this, let me quote the dictionary definition of remedial: *provided or intended for students who are experiencing learning difficulties.* It was a devastating blow. I knew I would have to hit the books as if my life depended on it. My future life did.

I'm starting to get some clarity about why I am writing and perhaps why you are reading. I was seven years old when my first life disaster happened. My parents moved in the middle of the school year, which forced me into a new school. I hated it. I hated it because I was happy where I was and loved my Hawaiian teacher. She praised my reading skills and made me feel smart. I was still playing with my friends from kindergarten and friends who lived on my street. My childhood response? I shut down. I was taken to a doctor (probably a psychologist) who asked me a lot of questions. I could sense that something was wrong. Adults whispered. The following school year, I was back in first grade, not second. Now I'm that kid who flunked first grade. The shame of it lasted all though elementary school, and for years afterward I felt less than whole. I'll be sharing some of the events of my life with the purpose of "paying it forward." If you can grow or be inspired by my challenges, I will have fulfilled the calling for writing this book.

How did I make it through my grueling undergraduate years and into the School of Veterinary Medicine at UC Davis? I applied myself 110 percent. No, I didn't need to read books about true grit; I just had it. The retarded first grader (yes, kids called me that and more) and the loser student that ended up in remedial college classes got into one of the most prestigious veterinary schools in the country. When you are faced with seemingly insurmountable circumstances in your life, odds not in your favor, and disappointing setbacks, but are still willing to go "all in" with both fists slugging, you will have found your own personal power. Use it. Passion is magic.

I kept my head down and studied. When I ran out of hours in the day, I set the alarm for a 4:00 a.m. wakeup call the next day. First stop was the donut shop to fuel up on coffee and a bear claw. I didn't care that it was a lousy breakfast; the warm smell of pastry and coffee was my reward for getting my ass out of bed and on the road by 5 a.m. Next stop was the college parking lot, finding a space to park under the brightest lamp post. With all distractions eliminated, my day started off with two full hours of study before classes started. I knew what I was up against. My grades would have to stand up to the challenge of a 3.5 grade point average or better. I gathered, by talking with other hopeful veterinary student candidates, that this was the first step in the elimination process for admission to medical school. Grades were followed by the standardized Graduate Record Examination (GRE) test scores, work experience, letters of recommendation, and a written narrative by all applicants explaining personal reasons for choosing to pursue a career in veterinary medicine. I never told them about Alf.

In my heart of hearts, I knew there were friends and family who, if they had to place a monetized bet, they would not be betting on me. Not even a fifty-fifty, heads or tails bet. But they didn't really know me and, honestly, neither did I. I knew that I could be stubborn—the human equivalent of a dog with a bone—because my Italian mother said I was. She called me *testardo* ("stubborn") when I made her angry. But I never understood why she referred to me as her gypsy daughter. It would be years into adulthood before I discovered my gypsy roots. I believe it was my mom's way of recognizing my fiercely independent spirit before I did. Always wanting things to go my way would later earn me the label of a control freak by some family members. But for this fight, I would need to find my Superwoman powers. There would be victories and defeats. Only James Harriot, the brave animal crusader, and my fairytale imagination kept me from quitting. There would be no white flag to wave. I was on a do or die mission.

Chapter Two

Mailbox

I've always made a total effort, even when the odds seemed entirely against me. I never quit trying; I never felt that I didn't have a chance to win.
—Arnold Palmer

The mailbox delivered the news I was waiting for. I don't remember the exact words in the letter of rejection. In fact, I didn't really expect a letter of acceptance. My application was timed to be filed as soon as I had enough college credits to apply for admission to the School of Veterinary Medicine at UC Davis. I basically had met the minimum requirements of college credits and one year of work experience. That was it. For me, the fight was just beginning. I would elicit feedback as to why I was not accepted and make the necessary tweaks. I would play the game. In review of my application, it was suggested that I expand my range of veterinary experience, bring up my GRE scores, and apply again the following year. I had snagged a job as a veterinary assistant, working with cats and dogs the previous year at a much lower pay grade, and quit a job that paid twice as much. Now I needed to broaden my veterinary experience and retake the GRE. Copy that.

I had the experience that comes with horse ownership all during my high school years. So I worked my contacts in the equine world until I found a veterinarian who would take me along on his calls once a week. Not only did I agree to work for free, I brought along home-baked bran muffins for our morning calls. He loved them, giving us a few things in common. I honestly had no interest or appetite for working with unpredictable animals of this size and strength. I had been bucked off, bitten, and stepped on by my own horse, and survived without permanent injuries. I had already crossed off farm animals and exotics from my list of no-no species. Just give me the cute, cuddly fur sort that meows or barks. But that needed to remain my little secret. The horse rides ended the day I received my letter of acceptance from UC Davis two years later. That vet, along with two other veterinarians, had written me letters of recommendation. One day, I would be asked to do the same. I made those recommendations letter-perfect. They would have to be.

As I mentioned before, the second piece of advice I received was to bring up my GRE scores. For this project, I needed extra help, knowing how lousy I perform on standardized tests. This was the hoop I hated trying to jump through. I did and still do believe this type of testing is a terrible method of judging someone's true abilities. If I had taken these types of test scores seriously in high school and again at the community college, I'd be working a hot dog stand at the local farmer's market. Instead, I paid my tuition for Stanley Kaplan courses and spent my weekends taking mock-up exams. It was painful and made the horse calls a walk in the park. I took the stupid test again and again until the scores were presumed to be average. I finally fell inside the bell curve.

I received my next letter of rejection the following year on a Friday afternoon. This was the punch to the gut you never forget. After I had boosted my hands-on experience to include equine work, improved my GRE test score, and boasted a GPA of 3.8 in all required science courses (the hard stuff, like chemistry and physics), did any of it matter? It was a weekend full of doubt, and defeat.

By Monday morning, discouragement had morphed into the red zone of anger. I felt cheated. I picked up the phone and made my second call to the university. This time it would not be a dry run as it had been before. It was a firm request to meet with the admissions review board. I wanted answers.

Several weeks later, with a packed suitcase, I drove over four hundred miles (eight hours with a pit stop) to arrive on the UC Davis campus. But there was no welcome mat waiting for me.

Sitting in a small office with all the warmth of a sterile operating room, I faced off with the man without a smile. In a rather stern voice, he pointed to a word that I had misspelled in my narrative. The word was *hydraulic*, and not one of a dozen well-educated people reading it had caught the deadly error before it reached the postman.

An insult like this would never happen today—bless the automated spellchecker. So there it was. He had no criticism other than the word *hydraulic*. What irony, considering the word was being used to describe a hydraulic lift table used to operate on horses. So much for my equine experience and the brownie points it supposedly earned me. I can't recall my verbal response, only the shame of it. To this day, I still question the validity of his finger pointing. Was the review board looking for any reason to disqualify applicants because they had so many, or had my application slipped through the cracks and never received an honest assessment by the review board? In either case, one of their faceless rejected applicants was now on campus asking questions. How convenient that I had provided them with the silver bullet to shoot me down. Four years of my life tossed away like waste paper. One misspelled word undid thousands of hours of study, working for peanuts, and my excellent letters of recommendations. (I know the letters were outstanding because the doctors proudly allowed me to read them.) Asking the admissions review board for any more winning advice would be like pinning the tail on a donkey—blind and stupid.

Pure logic was a good reason to quit. I had met all the requirements and more. What would be different about waiting another year and giving it another shot? Only one thing could make a difference—hiring a professional writer to review my next narrative. There could be no errors—not even a comma out of place.

So that's exactly what I did. I stayed in college, taking extra classes, and continued to work my veterinary job—with my eye on a vet school in the Philippines as a last resort. I had to believe the story was not over.

This time I knew when the letters had been mailed out. Once again, my fate would be delivered via postman. Every day brought anxiety. I was on trial waiting for the jury to deliver its verdict. Complete strangers would be making a life-changing decision about my future. I felt powerless. When the package arrived, I studied the outside envelope. I was looking for clues before I opened it, while trying to calm myself. Did it look different? Yes. Did it weigh more? Yes.

I don't remember how many times I read and re-read that acceptance letter. The next day I woke up in a panic, thinking I had dreamed the letter. I jumped out of bed, looking to find it. Only at that moment did I truly believe it was happening.

I was going to have a seat in the class of 1982. I wanted to call the man in the faraway land that set it all in motion. One day, I too would have stories to tell. I wanted them to be good ones.

Chapter Three

Vet School

Nothing in this world can take the place of persistence. Talent will not; nothing is more common than unsuccessful men with talent. Genius will not; unrewarded genius is almost a proverb. Education will not; the world is full of educated derelicts. Persistence and determination alone are omnipotent.
—Calvin Coolidge

Davis was a small college town; everything centered around the university. Coffee shops, cafés, and bikes were everywhere. For the first time in my life, I had moved away from family and friends—too far away for weekend visits. It was a lonely place for me, and my initial excitement faded over time. At the ripe age of twenty-eight, I was older than most of my classmates who went straight to college from high school. I often sat in the front rows and asked lots of questions during class. Little did I know that I had become the brunt of jokes by the "cool kids" seated in the back rows. Thinking about it now, years later, I can understand the angst I felt. It was a flashback to my first-grade shaming. The same kids who had teased me then were now young adults having their fun at my expense once again. I wanted to but could not admire all my classmates who had fought their own hard-won battles to enter the pearly gates of UC Davis. Jerks don't stop being jerks just because they get into a prestigious medical school. Copy that.

Nothing in college had prepared me for the backbreaking course load of medical school. The wagonloads of material to digest before exams felt like quicksand—barely keeping my head above water. After a full day of classes, I would get home in time to eat something and go to bed. The alarm was now set for 3:00 a.m.—time to get up and study. Catch up time was Saturdays and Sundays. How some of my classmates found time to party and do other things just made me feel more incompetent. I was homesick and miserable.

Here was the rotten truth waiting for me: Being a veterinary student is also a real hardship for devout animal lovers like myself. But people like me were only a handful in my class. Most students just breezed through the labs without thought about the animals being sacrificed to teach us. These furry lab rats were the homeless dogs and cats imprisoned at a local animal shelter. I was never able to justify the killing of unwanted shelter pets so that one day we could save the wanted population of pet dogs and cats. It all boiled down to just a matter of pet ownership—the haves and the have-nots. Perhaps it's different now, but I doubt it. I still feel the guilt of being part of it. So I had to keep telling myself that someday I would be saving lives. It was a matter of buying into that belief or dropping out. Which almost happened when I lied—but first the backstory.

I said it was a fact thirty-five years ago and it's even more relevant today. It's simply insane to continue to advance the notion that after four years of training, veterinary graduates can pass a state board exam declaring them competent to treat any animal other than humans. That we can put on white coats and treat horses, livestock (pigs, sheep, cows, goats, chickens), exotics (birds, snakes, guinea pigs, rabbits), and companion pets (dogs, cats). What's the problem? Every year there is a massive amount of new information in every field of medicine. Back in my day, addressing dental disease was the new kid on the block. It had never been taught before. The course load just got heavier, again.

To keep things in perspective, understand that the first veterinary school established in the United States was the Veterinary College of Philadelphia in 1852. Its purpose was to protect the public from infectious diseases through contaminated meat and to prevent losses of revenue for the farm industry. Animals were food, not pets. I did not go to veterinary school to work with livestock. By the time I was born, pets were becoming common place. I was not born on a farm in Kentucky. My motivation was to care for companion pets, nothing more. That was typical with my classmates as well—everyone was leaning in a specific direction prior to that first day of orientation. But inside the ivory tower, that didn't matter.

A much better approach would have been to let us choose our career path. In other words, basic training the first two years, and then choose among four tracks in the remaining two years: Separate tracks for equine, livestock, exotics, and companion animals to hone our skills. I even had a backup plan. Any time after graduation, you could return to study and become qualified in another area of veterinary medicine if you decided to branch out. It was a shared sentiment, but we the students had no voice.

To our minds, spending more hours of study and practice learning about fewer species would graduate us as more qualified doctors. After all, human docs only have one species to study. Think about that. I continued to harbor some pretty strong feelings on the subject even before I stepped into piles of cow dung.

I never blamed the cow that tried to kick me, wearing a gloved sleeve, before I rectally inserted my right arm up to my elbow to examine her bovine ovaries. They called it "food animal medicine" and I dreaded the eight-week rotation. I would become a key witness for the dark side of factory farming. Dairy cows standing in filthy conditions—painfully lame from rotting hooves. A florescent-lit windowless building with row after row of small crates called baskets. Five hens crammed into each basket, all piled on top of each other. They never saw sunlight and their claws never touched the ground. There was no fox in this steel-encased henhouse. My strategy was to lay low and use up any sick time I could get away with. It almost worked.

When I caught wind that one of our field trips was to visit a slaughterhouse, it would be my food animal last straw. Apparently, I was not the only compassionate soul feeling the dread. A few days before the planned visit, a shattering announcement was made: No student would be excused for any reason. "Better get your boots on." Okay, that was the announcement. But then the announcement was followed by a dire warning: Anyone planning to ditch the trip would be subject to school expulsion. The ruling dinosaurs just shook my earth.

My move to vegetarianism—spurred by animal-cruelty factory-farming methods—made the direct order feel more like my own death sentence. Damage my psyche with terrifying sounds, foul smells, and horrifying visuals, or take the risk of being kicked out of veterinary school. It was never a question. People who are compelled to act on personal principles that cannot be violated must take risks—sometimes the biggest risk of all. It's not something that can be decided, like, should I move to this or that state? Take this or that job? Buy this or that house? Those are pros and cons that carry weight. So, when I was called into the director's office, I lied. In the end, they had no proof that my story wasn't true. I should have been nominated for an Oscar.

UC Davis School of Veterinary Medicine was a four-year survival course. Two years of an intense Marine-like boot camp followed by two years in the battlefield. Unlike me, most soldiers seemed to weather the good with the bad. Then there were a few rare birds who seemed to thrive. No one was surprised when Valarie was awarded valedictorian upon graduation. On every subject, she took detailed and perfectly penned notes that she organized into a small binder to bring during hospital rounds. A wrong answer never came out of her month. She was pretty, soft-spoken and kind to everyone—making it impossible not to like her. So I had to settle for admiration and dismiss every envious thought I had. Oh, how I wanted those notes.

Valarie thrived until sometime after graduation, when it was time to be out in the real world and get a job. Two years later she was teaching biology to high school students. What? The girl most admired and "most likely to succeed"? After talking with a classmate who had been working in the same veterinary practice with Valerie in Los Angeles, some clues were revealed. Sadly, her fall from grace might have been predicted. She was more brain than brawn. Grades don't really matter in the real world.

Vet school survival included a curriculum that made finals week a walking nightmare. The last week of every quarter would end with five consecutive days of testing. I crammed like crazy and held my breath for passing scores—settling for a C average. Many of us looked like zombies by the end of the week. Only to repeat the cycle again and again every year until it was time for the all-day exam. The big one: the state board examination.

None of us flunked out of vet school in the class of '86, but some would flunk the state board exam and would not be going on job interviews that summer. They would take the test again after discovering their weak areas and finally pass. Flunking first grade—although the circumstances were entirely different—was rearing its ugly head. I would not be whispered about again twenty-five years later.

Chapter Four

Petey

It's okay to be scared. Being scared means you're about to do something really, really brave.
—Mandy Hale

My big plan to pass the state board exam was to hunker down and gorge on whatever junk food I craved. That way, I would not be interrupted by hunger during endless hours of memorization. As a bonus, the boxes of See's candies (the turtles were my favorites) served as my ongoing positive reinforcement tool. This trick worked. Like an obedient dog, I performed. After months of intense study, and a full nine years after I announced my do or die mission, I was a do and done it. I could not wait to pick out matching frames for my university diploma and California state license. But I had no plan to hang them anywhere. Not yet.

In a near state of exhaustion, I had only one thing on my mind—to get the hell out of university town and take the lab-rat canine, Petey, with me. I had met another survivor. Before you meet Petey, I need to tell you about the dark side of veterinary teaching.

Every year, a new collection of unwanted shelter dogs arrives in a van. When their time is up at the shelter, they become the property of the teaching hospital, to be used as guinea pigs for "wet labs." Each third-year student is assigned their own lab dog. At first, I would take my assigned dog out on the weekends for some exercise, but the guilt became overwhelming. Once outside, I wanted to let her go—at least she would have a chance. Even roadkill was better than being stuck in a cage 24/7. All the lab dogs were confined in cages in what looked to be an old storage room. No kennels and not even a single window. You could hear frantic barking and rattling cages before you even opened the door. I dreaded that room and the desperation. My lab dog was a border collie mix. Her freedom would come at the end of a needle after all the wet labs had been completed, her limp body carried out in a black trash bag. Nobody wanted to talk about it. I suspect it was a budget issue and not a flat-out effort to embark on animal abuse. But that didn't make it okay. After the disgusting food animal rotation a year earlier, it was clear. Animals had only one purpose at the teaching hospital: Alive and dead cadavers to study.

It was an institution without a heart. And it wasn't just the heartless food animal industry. When it came time for us to follow around the residents, working with real patients (dogs and cats with devoted owners), it was the moment I had dreamed of. It was time to play doctor—something I had actually fantasized about and role played as a child.

The white coats had gathered in the treatment room where a dog was being prepped for a bone marrow biopsy. Soon after the procedure began, so did the screams. If the dog had been given a local anesthetic (which I cannot recall), it did nothing to stop the immense pain. The more the dog struggled, the heavier the restraint. I couldn't take it. When I objected and demanded to know why the resident did not give the poor dog something more to stop the pain, she shot back. "You'd better toughen up or get out of this room," was her answer. Did she really think her heartless warning was going to toughen me up? I was tough enough to get this far. That was all the "tough" I needed.

During my twenty-five-year career, I never compromised an animal's wellbeing by not relieving its pain or suffering—and I never hesitated to do so. There was absolutely no medical reason not to medicate that screaming dog. Screw my *alma mater*—I wasn't one of them. They never saw a penny despite years of sending me letters and requests for donations. I had made a few good friends and they would serve as my only fond memories. My wish for that resident was to find her ass at the business end of a biopsy needle one day.

I first met Petey in the hallway of the teaching hospital—at first, I thought he was a patient. He was wearing some type of monitoring device strapped around his chest. As I stopped to stoop down and greet the handsome pit bull, I learned he was not a patient after all. He was a lab dog being used by the cardiac department to conduct testing. *What?*

After doing some investigation, I found the ward that housed Petey and ten of his inmates, all kept in separate kennels on a different hospital floor. So why were Petey and his inmates not euthanized after one year of vet student practice labs? They took it. Remarkably, Petey and his kennel club dogs didn't break. They did not become aggressive or bite anyone. They remained workable and not difficult to restrain. They didn't go batshit crazy. Petey helped me cope with a powerless situation. I signed him out for long walks and talks. I told him again and again we would leave together. I had a plan.

Petey jumped into the front seat of a rented U-Haul without question. In a matter of minutes, the truck rolled off campus and Petey became stolen property. It was another risk

I had to take. Months earlier, I requested permission from the teaching hospital to adopt him after graduation. But one other dog had been there longer than Petey—a German shepherd. Sarah had logged a full eight years behind bars as university property. I was granted permission to take her, not Petey. My Petey only had six years under his collar. It was truly heartbreaking, but I made a promise to Petey. I told him the final date we were getting the hell out. I don't break promises. But I do break rules.

Chapter Five

Home, Sweet Home

Ethics is knowing the difference between what you have a right to do and what is right to do.
—Potter Stewart

The eight-hour drive back to my hometown felt like a jailbreak. Petey and I would be free from the rules and expectations that governed our everyday lives. Every mile distanced us further from institutional grayness devoid of any compassion. I cried tears of relief as I drove that U-Haul truck south along highway I-5 for the last time. My final trip home without a return ticket. A home with a real bed for Petey and a yard, with trees, for us to play in.

During that last year, when I pledged my full commitment to Petey, I had found another secret weapon. I would spend my free time living in the future. The daily daydream was all about the house I would claim and redecorate when I moved back. The moment my parents promised to sell me one of their rental houses, I knew the one. I still remembered it from my teenage years when I was helping Mom clean the rental houses. I also knew that I would do battle with Dad. You see, I wanted the only house my landlord father did not want to sell.

I never made it easy for Dad. As a real estate broker, he bragged about being a good negotiator—and he was. He was a real dealmaker and he did very well for his family. When Dad told me it was a no-go on the house I picked, I put my own set of negotiator genes to the test. I really empathized with dear old Dad; he had good reasons to keep that tenant in the house I wanted. Maria was his best renter and Dad was very fond of her. She had been in that house for more than ten years, taking good care of it and paying rent on time. When I did not surrender, Dad pulled out his final weapon. He would tell Maria to move under one condition: I would have to be standing right next to him as he knocked on the door and dropped the bomb. I agreed. Yep, the ungrateful first-born child was in the hot seat—and rightfully so. I had been spoiled by his devotion. I never wanted for anything, and I loved him to the moon.

I'm not sure my dad understood that the house was more to me than just a house, but my mother did. I was at the end of my emotional rope and just knowing that house was waiting for me kept me hanging on. On the occasional weekend trip home, I looked at carpet, furniture and paint colors. I could visualize my new life and how everything was going to look. It was a very big carrot.

As my arrival date got closer, Mom got a head start on the cleanup. My boyfriend joined in on the weekends when he could. As told to me by him, Dad lost another fight when my mom took him on. This time it was about carpet. Dad was on the side of getting the decades-old carpets cleaned, not removed. Being the youngest child of poor immigrant farmers from Czechoslovakia no doubt had taught him the value of being frugal. For better or worse, he married a hot-blooded, beautiful, big-busted Italian—raised with upper middle-class status. This financial polarity was at the root of most arguments witnessed by me and my two sisters. So here was mom's carpet response: "Rip it out, I know my daughter!" Beautiful shades of gray Berber carpet awaited my arrival—just what the doctor ordered!

I spent a lot of time on a cozy couch (one of many wedding gifts) napping in my new living room. The look and smell of that Berber was proof positive that I was in a land far, far away from that university town. House decorating would become my therapy for the next three months. It was all I had the enthusiasm for, and I wasn't interested in much else. While my shiny new colleagues were out looking for jobs or starting internships, I was on the couch watching *Oprah*. I needed time to do nothing other than cleaning that house, once again.

When I finally came back to life, I started to review my options. I settled for the most familiar, despite my gut feelings about him. His lack of boundaries set off a creepy vibe. Dr. RK was one of several vets I had worked with at a large veterinary hospital during my pre-vet years. He started trying to recruit me when I was still a student at UC Davis, so I was not surprised when he started calling again after I moved back into the area. I remained reluctant until he offered to set up a lunch date for me to meet Patty, one of his associates. My plan was to drill Patty for dirt at lunch, but she didn't give me any. She was actually quite charming.

I really liked Patty and we worked well together, but it wasn't long before I realized that I had been lured into the spider's web. Unethical RK and I ended up duking it out. I quit before the third round got started. After handing him my thirty-day resignation, he fired me. He landed the final punch. Gone were my plans to finish up with my patients and say my goodbyes. That was when I knew I would never work for anyone again. I don't take orders from people I don't respect—another attribute I inherited from my Sinatra-loving "I do it my way" father.

Dear old Dad understood my dilemma. He was a real estate broker with his own office and agents—the boss. I doubt that he realized that he was raising his daughter to be one, too. So, the bank of Terifaj loaned me all the money I needed. In eager beaver style, I leased a space, designed and finished the build-out, and opened a fully equipped hospital in less than one year. Yep, I did it *my way* working the night shifts at an emergency clinic and picking up daytime relief work. Yes, it was a crazy time. But this time *I* was in control, not the greedy RK or a threatening hospital administration demanding compliance. What did I know about running a business? Absolutely nothing.

"Nothing" is an expensive proposition. The first five years left me debilitated with clouds of doubt and heavy debt. In fact, I knew I was in trouble the first year. Looking back, trouble was headed my way when my veterinary career took a sharp detour. My all-time goal was to become a rock-star vet, not a business owner. "Save lives and make the world a better place" was my mantra. So, I skipped the business class being offered in our senior year, telling myself that rock-star vets are not business people—the rant of naiveté. No, I would seek out mentors and work with accomplished veterinarians to hone my doctor skills. I pictured myself taking center stage to tackle every mystery illness like a detective. No case would go unsolved. I'd figure out the diagnosis and find the cure. That rock star opportunity got me a pink slip when I could not reconcile myself to find another job. I would learn the hard way. Life would teach me.

And it wasn't just the RK turn-off. I had already experienced the workings of several outdated veterinary hospitals while doing relief work. The lack of cleanliness and smelly odors were appalling. Next, I rested my sights on the disorganization of cluttered spaces without windows—guaranteed eye strain and headaches from bright fluorescent lights. The nail in the coffin came when I knew I'd be dealing with policies I am strongly opposed to, like this shocker: I had never seen a request for "convenience euthanasia" (based on issues like owners moving, pets peeing in the house and other correctable behavior problems, and the unwanted pets of deceased relatives) be denied. Never.

Sure, I had lots of good reasons to avoid getting another job. I had lots of good reasons why I should be the boss and write the rules. At my hospital, there would be no convenient drop-off euthanasia's. No one was going to just drop off a dog or cat they didn't want for any reason. Rule Number One: All euthanasia procedures had to be authorized by the doctor, which required a doctor/patient relationship. Period. The experienced staff that I would eventually hire took notice. It was perhaps their first clue that I was a different breed. My hospital. My ethics. It was the only thing I really had going for me.

Part Two
Career

Chapter Six

Death and the Curiosity that Saved Cats

Experience is simply the name we give our mistakes.
—Oscar Wilde

It was a new hire who sounded the first alarm bell. But first came the odd request that I meet her and her partner over drinks. (Maybe it was dinner as well. My memory is foggy.) After I received apparent partner approval that night, and a few days before this gal was to start work, I got the weird phone call. She wanted to know about health insurance coverage. This raised a flag in my mind. When I started to explain to her that the job did not include benefits (I was barely able to cover payroll), she became insistent and began to explain to me why insurance expenses were necessary in operating my business. Well, that bossy gal got herself fired before I could politely end the call. I can't remember the names of these two entitlement queens, but the lesson lived on. I got better and better at finding good hires. When Janet came on, I had found the golden goose. (You'll meet Janet in another chapter.)

Then the second alarm bell rang. My clinical inexperience, compounded by being the lone doctor, was the perfect storm for unpleasant learning experiences that still haunt me. When things went wrong—things that I determined later a more experienced doctor might have avoided—the mind games from hell started, as if mental punishment was a guarantee it would never happen again. It made me both hypervigilant and a little paranoid. At times when I would confess to colleagues, they told me their horror stories. It only worried me more to think I was so vulnerable. So I added their sins to my list of how to avoid another disaster.

Finally, the day came when a routine dental cleaning went bad. My patient was a beautiful, silky black feline. Following standard protocol, an IV catheter was placed, anesthesia was induced, and the cat was intubated. The heart EKG monitor was on and beeping. Not a single hiccup. As I was adjusting the IV drip flow, I noticed an eerie silence. As the technician checked the electrodes for a loose connection, I had my stethoscope in my ears, hovering over a furry chest, desperately listening for a heartbeat. Dead silence. We jumped into frantic CPR activity in a total state of disbelief. The cat had died before we, the paramedics, could intervene. There was no foul play, no one to blame. I didn't know if I would survive.

The owner was at work after dropping the cat off that morning. It was the last time she would see her beloved cat alive. It was the first time I would make an unexpected phone call to deliver terrible news. I never imagined I would make a call like that. Thinking about it only made it worse, so I forced myself to just pick up the damn phone. I didn't have a rehearsed announcement dressed up with my apologies. As soon as I identified myself, I let out my grief over what had just happened. I spoke to Ann as if we were friends sharing the death of a loved one. There was no doctor talk. As I started to speak, the floodgate of tears opened wide. The brief conversation ended when I could no longer hold back the sobs. Nothing had prepared me for that day; nothing could have.

Later, my doctor brain would kick in to offer a possible explanation, hoping to point the finger somewhere. I knew that sudden-death episodes were often blamed on undetected cardiac disease (heart failure). Cats are infamous for cardiomyopathy—a disease of the heart muscle. It is much less common now since the discovery of a taurine deficiency in commercial diets. The necessary amount of taurine (an essential amino acid in meat, required to prevent nutritional diseases) was a miscalculation by AAFCO (Association of American Feed Control Officials). Otherwise known as a guesstimate. (More about AAFCO in Chapter Eleven.)

In the 1970s, researchers showed that a taurine deficiency can cause degeneration of the retina in cats, a leading cause of feline blindness. During my final year in vet school, an astute cardiology resident, Dr. Paul D. Pion, stumbled on the link between heart disease and blindness caused by low levels of taurine in blood samples of cats eating commercial diets. At the time, Pion was primarily studying cats that had developed dilated cardiomyopathy (heart failure),and noticed that some of the cardiac patients referred to him for treatment also showed signs of retinal disease. Curiosity led him to question if there was a possible connection between both diseases. The bombshell answer—*Yes!*—came after he confirmed that all fifty of his cardiac patients were also suffering from low levels of taurine. The cure was as simple as providing taurine supplementation. Dr. Pion's research successfully reversed this cardiac disease and forced the pet food industry to provide higher levels of taurine in their diets. So everyone would be left to ponder just how many cats did this man-made disease (the cause was not discovered until the late 1980s) send to the grave. Of course there is no way to actually tally that death toll. Had the black lifeless cat on my treatment table been a victim of the pet food industry? I'll never know, and neither will Ann. I can only hope for her forgiveness.

After that doomsday event, I could no longer trust calling anything that required anesthesia "a routine procedure." Doubt and fear became my daily companions; you don't learn about doubt and fear in vet school. You are either watching or being watched. The life of a patient does not hang over your head. But I was eight hundred miles away from the kingdom of a teaching hospital. It was the real world now and reality had just kicked my ass. I had to find a way to translate my doubt and fear into acceptable risk.

First, I had to challenge the veterinary dogma that surrounded dental care. Having your pet's teeth cleaned (a dental procedure) was listed under the auspices of licensed veterinary care. Sometime in the 1990s, a decade later, some enterprising groomers had added a new service—oral hygiene. Most commonly, they offered teeth brushing. But others went so far as to try to scale off tartar too. That kicked off a hot debate and the veterinary profession was up in arms. Ironically, what drove many pet owners to seek unqualified dental care was driven by the veterinary recommendations we were all prescribing. Let me back up a bit.

The vet school curriculum had finally recognized the neglect of dental care in small animal medicine right around the time I was a third-year veterinary student. This new dive into pet dentistry was emerging to educate both veterinarians and their vet techs in how to perform proper dental care. An oral exam, thorough cleaning, and extractions, if needed, were to be performed only under general anesthesia. At the time, this made perfect sense to me. Hands and instruments invading the mouths of carnivores with sharp teeth did not appeal to me. And, of course, all veterinarians had patients that would not allow it.

I sung the virtues of routine dental cleaning as a foundational part of practicing preventative medicine. Removing tartar, and keeping it off, was the only way to prevent gum infections that progressed to diseased teeth needing to be extracted. Advanced disease leads to more misery for your pet and your pocketbook. So I made it a habit to look into the mouth of every patient during all routine and other examinations. Not a day went by when multiple recommendations for dental procedures became scheduled future appointments. After every dental procedure, pet owners were sent home with goody bags of special pet toothpaste, the proper-sized toothbrush, and instructions on how to brush. Instructions were topped off with a warning that went something like this: "If you don't brush Susie's teeth every day, she will need her teeth cleaned again with anesthesia every 6 – 12 months." So the onus was placed smack-dab on the pet owner's shoulders.

You can see how the growing demand for home dental care might morph itself into an extension of grooming. Enterprising groomers tried to tap that market. However, the offer to brush teeth during a grooming session every six to eight weeks was not the answer. It was two infrequent for tartar prevention and completely ineffective for pets with visible tartar and gingivitis. When I caught wind of clients opting in for dental grooming services, heads rolled.

Follow-up dental care at home was problematic for pet owners for several reasons. Brushing teeth is not something our pets understand or appreciate, making the chore difficult. Adding the time factor for this new daily chore during a busy work day compounded the high rate of non-compliance. Failure to manage home care increases the need for general anesthesia. Anesthesia makes up about 75 percent of the total cost to clean teeth—a hefty price tag. Lastly, pet owners rightly expressed their worry about putting their pet "under."

Despite these negatives, in a few short years public awareness of the need for dental care had really taken off. Then someone opened the grooming Pandora's box. I suspect it was an enterprising vet tech who saw the need and opportunity. With time, under the guidance of a human dental hygienist, techniques were mastered to scale off tarter using the same dental instruments in veterinary patients without anesthesia. While many of my colleagues bemoaned these renegade dental techs with screams about safety and competence, I could smell the fear of lost veterinary revenues.

I had a different pet safety issue: the risk of another fatal dental cleaning. After careful observation and a few tweaks (scaling the teeth of staff pets, including my own dogs), I hired the hybrid vet tech/dental hygienist. More of my patients got their teeth cleaned and more often. I insisted on mild sedation to keep them calm and reduce any risk of injury. It worked like a charm. From then on, anesthesia was used only when the dental vet tech or doctor found diseased teeth that needed to be extracted. It was a win-win for pets and dental revenues in my practice. If only the new "sedated but still awake dental cleaning" had been an option, that black cat might have gone home with her owner that afternoon.

Note: "If only" is a toxic can of uncertainty. Don't open it.

Chapter Seven

Survival

Nobody talks of entrepreneurship as survival, but that's exactly what it is and what nurtures creative thinking.
—Anita Roddick

I was finally running from second to third base, but with no guarantee I'd victoriously slide safely into home. Along with my professional self-doubts and setbacks came the monthly expenses: rent, an SBA loan, invoices for hospital supplies, insurance, utilities, payroll costs and more. Bills that mounted up to a big monthly nut to crack, and no paycheck waiting for me. For the first six months, after the celebratory ribbon cutting, I suffered the humiliation of asking Dad for more money. I was coming up short about five thousand dollars each month, and not even paying a penny on the substantial $150,000 family loan that covered the costs of the hospital buildout. That first year, Dad wrote checks for my debt bailout until my mother stepped in and said no more. Nothing could have prepared me for that earthquake. I felt abandoned by my parents for the first time in my life—my village destroyed. I felt physically trapped under the emotional weight of the rubble – my spirit broken. Knowing I was in for the fight of my life, my survival instincts took over.

I bargained with vendors to extend my credit and made minimum payments. Whenever that didn't work, I just didn't pay. My landlord was no cupcake either, so I had to gamble that he would not start legal action as long as I was honest with him and paid something every month; this bought me a little more time. I had to start thinking like a businesswoman—a real one. When expenses exceed revenues, going out of business becomes a harsh reality. Somehow, I managed to keep the lights on.

My landlord wasted no time in setting me straight. Along with all his impressive real estate holdings, he owned an envelope company, of all things. There was something Texan about him, or maybe it was just that he was tall and dressed more like a cowboy—hat, buckle and boots. So when I proposed that he lower my rent, he "gunned" me down quickly. That's when he explained how it worked in his envelope business. In a dismissive tone, he simply said, "Stop trying to cut your expenses and increase your prices." In a moment of defeat, the light bulb went on. I had to start working the other end of the math equation—up the revenue or die. Going out of business is the definition of defeat.

Against my better judgment, I jumped on the vaccine clinic bandwagon. It was the late 1980's and lots of my colleagues were already doing it. I felt the competitive need to join them. Saturdays began with morning appointments from 9 a.m. until noon. The vaccine parade started at 1 p.m. This went on for several months until I had my come-to-Jesus moment. I had allowed desperation to violate my better judgment. My attempt to justify this source of "funny money" would never build the practice I envisioned, nor did it support any dialogue that focused on enhanced health care management. My emphasis on the importance of annual physical exams, better diets, natural supplements, and routine dental care had nothing in common with yearly booster vaccinations. In fact, the very subject surrounding the need for annual vaccinations was stirring a lot of hot debate in the veterinary community. And I had already developed a healthy mistrust for pharmaceutical reps selling the new so-called "miracle vaccine" or drug of the year.

In the real world, mailing out yearly vaccine reminders to drum up more business had nothing to do with actual science. It was simply good for business and researchers would ultimately win that debate (details in Chapter Thirteen). But when the alarm bells started going off, I dropped the routine protocol of annual vaccinations like a hot potato.

First came the scare that some cats were developing cancerous or malignant tumors (medical term *fibrosarcoma*) at the vaccine injection site. That was followed by some rather radical advice to change the injection site to a rear leg, instead of under the loose skin of the neck, in case of tumor development. That way the entire leg could be amputated to prevent the spread of cancer. Good grief!

In addition to the cancer scare, pioneering researchers demonstrated how vaccines were capable of setting off a multitude of potentially fatal autoimmune diseases such as hemolytic anemia (the abnormal destruction of red blood cells). More commonly witnessed, a whacky immune response could also lead to chronic conditions such as food and skin allergies.

We must all grapple with the fact that vaccines invoke an inflammatory response by the immune system, not strictly limited to the diseases they aim to prevent. Any condition tagged as an "itis"—such as arthritis; pancreatitis; colitis; encephalitis and so on—can be unintended consequences. Without a doubt, vaccines do carry risks, but they are also necessary. Vaccine protocols and the determination of which vaccines are appropriate depend on several factors. Age, efficacy, and likelihood of exposure to the pathogen are all considerations. So choose wisely for that sleeping cat on your bed and that coach potato dog on your sofa. Urban house pets need annual exams, not more vaccines. You need to challenge any vet that says otherwise.

Ultimately, I did what was best for every pet entrusted to my care. I had to trust that, in time, it would pay off. So I spent the extra time to educate my clients, offered wellness plans in lieu of vaccine reminders, and explained why I recommended vaccine titers (measures of antibodies in the blood, providing proof of disease immunity). People will pay for value and shoppers will shop around. I decided to sell value. I still had a lot to figure out, and for a while questioned whether or not my parents had truly failed me. Maybe I had failed them.

The standoff ended after a conversation I had with one of my clients while treating her ill cat. (I believe that health professionals often share territory with bartenders. People talk to us about lots of stuff.) This likable lady (of my generation) wanted to tell me about her parents. Her painful regrets spoke volumes to me. Oddly, she had no idea about my parental situation. I listened, waited a few weeks, and eventually called home. I didn't want my story to end as my cat-lady client's had. And it didn't.

However, it would be years before I could retire the painful rejection I felt from my mother. I really thought it was all about the money, and that she cared more about her bank account than me. As the years passed, I wondered if there was another explanation. Perhaps she had another motive besides the monetary one, motivation that was more in line with the "tough love" camp. Was mom willing to make a high-stakes bet that her eldest daughter would not drown after she had harpooned her leaky lifeboat? It would be nearly a decade later before Mom would ultimately win that bet.

Chapter Eight

Lucky Charm

Fate controls who walks into your life, but you decide who you let walk out, who you let stay, and who you refuse to let go.
—Anonymous

In the beginning of my fledgling veterinary career, the hospital worked me six days a week and demanded that I be on call every Sunday. This went on until I hooked up with a relief vet I liked. I hired Dr. SC based more on a wing and a prayer than any financial sense it made. I was desperate for a day off.

It was a Tuesday morning just after waking up. First, I realized that my alarm had not gone off. Moments later, when I was fully conscious, the realization hit me. Another doctor was on duty today, not me. I stayed in bed to stare at the ceiling and reassure myself it was true. Today, inside the fortress of my bedroom walls, I was free from all hospital responsibilities and duties. Ten hours of alone time felt like heaven. The smoke from my burnout was undeniable. SC agreed to stay on one day each week. And on those days, I watched soap operas and ate ice cream. That was my therapy. It kept me in the marriage, so to speak.

When I finally did manage to run my business into the black, it had nothing to do with luck. But I do believe in lucky charms, and I was about to find one.

Janet was a newbie Registered Veterinary Technician (RVT) graduate who had just passed her California state exam. Her previous work experience as a zookeeper lacked the hands-on field experience of a veterinary hospital—a requirement needed to complete her course work. As I recall, several months before graduation, Janet responded to a want-ad one of my employees had posted on a college bulletin board. We needed an extra pair of hands to assist Christine, our only RVT at the time. During the interview, Janet explained to Christine that she just wanted an opportunity to work in the veterinary field to satisfy a requirement for graduation. Christine offered to take her on as a volunteer until she logged the required number of hours needed. It was a short-term relationship that would later bear fruit. Fortunately, after graduation, Janet decided not to return to the wild kingdom. She wanted something less wild and crazy.

My practice would become Janet's first paid job working in a veterinary hospital. I wish that I could take full credit for hiring Janet, but it was Christine (another superb catch and fellow escapee from Dr. X) who brought her on board as our second RVT. Janet was rather quiet and somewhat shy. So, I had not taken much notice of her while she was working her volunteer hours. I didn't even know her last name. Mom always liked to say, "Still waters run deep." Janet was deep.

The first thing that caught my eye was that Janet was always doing something. Perhaps it's the reason she didn't talk all that much. At some point, it occurred to me that Janet did not take breaks either. It was more important to her that all tasks be completed on time. She was living proof of the saying that if you want something done, go ask a busy person. It didn't matter what I asked Janet to do; she was always ready to tackle it. Over time, I handed off more and more administrative work and other unwanted tasks, like talking with drug reps. Within two years Janet was wearing the shoes of a full-time hospital manager who could also function as an RVT whenever needed. I was the envy of all my colleagues, who spent more time complaining about their staff than some of their clients. Janet raised the bar. No one ever raised it higher.

Eventually, I had my dream team: A staff that scored all A's and B's. I quickly let go of the few C's, and D's I had managed to hire. This, I believe, helped me avoid one of the biggest mistakes employers make. They keep the C's on. The justification that they are "not bad enough to fire" is gutless. Your A's and B's will resent them and the team will not pull together when the road gets rocky. You will lose your "lucky charms." Thankfully, I never lost mine. Janet stayed with me until I faced my retirement year. The same year she got pregnant—with twins! Only fate could have separated us. Fate finally did.

Chapter Nine

Denver

I ask you to judge me by the enemies I have made.
—Franklin D. Roosevelt

Reading newspapers was not my thing. Doom and gloom headlines were daily blasts of more bad news. "Who needs that crap?" was my response. I received and delivered daily doses of bad news just by showing up for work. I didn't want to pile on more, reading about tragic plane crashes, sexual abuse and gang shootings. My small world needed to stay centered around my veterinary duties, staff and clients. I didn't think I could cope with much else. But that was all about to change.

Recently I had redesigned my office space to create desk space for Janet, making it easier for us to confide in each other and work together on projects. Busy-bee Janet always arrived at work before I did, and I'd come in every morning to find her sitting at her desk catching up on paperwork. But not this morning. Janet had been waiting to hand me a newspaper. Denver, Colorado, was front-page headline news. I had no idea that Denver and other city councils around the country had been voting in favor of banning so-called "pit bulls." In fact, "pit bull" isn't a breed; it's a slang term used to describe the American Pit Bull Terrier, the Bull Terrier, the American

Staffordshire Terrier, and the Staffordshire Bull Terrier—or some combination thereof. In a matter of seconds my dumbfounded expression turned into rage. Janet had tears in her eyes while I was seeing all shades of red.

Denver's ban had been passed in 1989—sixteen years earlier—but could not be enforced. It came on the heels of two human attacks by dogs deemed, at that time, to be pit bulls. Followed by an outpouring of public outrage, the fix was in. The jury of public opinion voted to condemn all bully type dogs based on breed alone. It was an ignorant and blatant refusal to consider relevant factors relating to dog behavior—a knee-jerk reaction to a social problem, one of irresponsible dog ownership and stud-like status.

Let me explain the dark history of powerful-looking dogs. Before the bully breeds got popular with the thugs and other lowlife's, they had the Doberman and the Rottweiler. Sometime in the eighties, the muscular bullies became the new bad ass dog. That stigmatization was the kiss of death for the popular family dog of the forties—America's most beloved breed. If you didn't already know that, google some photo shots from the era.

In its neglect for fact-finding and expert testimony, the city sued its own state of Colorado in May 2004, arguing the law violated Denver's home rule. A judge ruled for Denver, allowing the ban to be enforced. The mayhem that followed is best told by Sonya Dias. Denver's irrational bully ban made Gryffindor, and thousands of others like him, targets for extermination.

As reported by ABC News
Ban Has Denver Pit Bulls Marked for Death
By Dean Schabner July 27, 2005

For Sonya Dias, when the choice came down to leaving the city she loved and the Victorian home she had painstakingly restored or giving up her dog, there was no contest.

Her house is on the market and her bags are packed, because Denver says she cannot keep her beloved pet, a pit bull named Gryffindor. After several high-profile pit bull attacks, the city enacted a law banning the breed, but Dias insists concern about her pet is unwarranted.

"He's just a big old dork, a slobbering lummox of a dog," Dias said. "I don't see how he's a danger to anybody."

Because of Denver's 1989 ban on pit bulls, Gryffindor would have likely been collected by animal control officers and killed. The city has been enforcing the law with a vengeance since May 9, when the state Supreme Court allowed the ordinance to stand despite a state law barring breed-specific bans.

Already, the city has rounded up at least 380 pit bulls and killed at least 260 of them, according to documents that opponents of the ban obtained under a Freedom of Information request.

"Some of the family dogs they had in the back yard and they [animal control officers] climbed over the fence and nabbed them," said Dias, who works as a loan officer at a mortgage company. "Some they came to the door, and people didn't know they didn't have to let animal control into the house without a warrant."

At first, Dias decided to become a criminal to keep her dog. She hid Gryffindor, hoping to be able to keep both her home and her best friend. But that didn't last.

"I am not cut out for a life on the lam," she said. "I put my house on the market, found a beautiful sanctuary [for Gryffindor] and now my cousin has him outside the city limits."

"I just can't believe this is the best thing they could think of for dealing with dangerous dogs," Dias said.

"The symptom keeps changing. Do they really think the drug dealers won't just find another dog—Rottweilers or Labrador retrievers?"

A few months later, I would meet Sonya at the Denver airport. But the battle cry started that morning reading Janet's newspaper; I was Sonya's ally before we even met. Janet helped track her down and we talked over the phone several times before I flew to Colorado. Sonya said her top priority was raising money for legal fees to fight the ban. At that time, I had organized a dog walking club that met on Sunday mornings in a local park. We had come together to petition our city to build a dog park. I would share this breaking news with them that same week in the park. I remember standing on top of a redwood picnic table to gather my flock around. Without a pleasant greeting or smile, I started to speak. As soon as my voice became shaky, I saw the look of panic on their faces. I felt my initial outrage melt into complete despair. Before I could finish my announcement and plea for help, the Kleenex came out. Hands reached for me and helped me down from the table. I sat on the grass and cried for the first time since that morning with Janet and the newspaper story. I was ready to fight—and so were the Sunday dog walkers.

It only took nine people to pledge all monies from a weekend garage sale for us to send Sonya a check for two thousand dollars. It wasn't a lot of money, but it was just enough for Sonya and her friends to retain a lawyer. They were somewhat flabbergasted to have that kind of support from total strangers, but we weren't really strangers at all. We were fellow dog-lovers, just like them. And we all owned a bully breed or knew someone who did. It was about as personal as it gets. They called us their "California Angels."

It would be my first—but not my last—trip to the Mile High City in Colorado. I just had to meet and hug these dog warriors. As the plane landed and announced our arrival to the Denver International Airport, I thought of Petey. Denver had become a death camp of breed discrimination for dogs that looked like my dog. I'd rather live on Mars.

On the car ride to my hotel, Sonya talked non-stop. She told story after story of what was happening and to whom it was happening. Animal control officers were given free rein to knock on doors and take away family dogs. Neighbors turned in their neighbor's pets. All stray dogs (including lost dogs) that fit sketchy descriptions of the outlawed bully breeds were confiscated and destroyed—whether they wore dog tags or not. She showed me a picture of a Boxer that the Denver shelter euthanized simply because it fit a few of the physical traits of a Bulldog—as did many of the mixed breeds. When she started on the story about Forrest, I asked her to stop. I could not hear another word. Not at that point. I checked into my hotel and went straight to the bar. I'd skip the wine and order cocktails. I needed hard liquor.

When Forrest was picked up as a lost dog, his family would fight to get him back. For a backup small army, they had Sonya's small band of warriors, some local supporters, and now they had me and their California Angels. We were a motley crew fueled by outrage. If there had been more of us, it could have become a mob scene. Sonya sent us a video of a twenty-something kid standing in front of the Denver shelter pleading for the release of his dog. This committed guy vowed to camp out at the shelter every day during daylight hours after the authorities denied the release of his beloved dog, Forrest.

There was no rhyme or reason to any of it. Forrest's family lived on the outskirts of Denver residing in Littleton County.

The story that unfolded would never have happened if Forrest had not wandered off into "enemy territory," crossing the county line, where he was picked up by Denver's animal control. He quickly passed Denver's moronic evaluation and was deemed to be a god-awful pit bull. Suddenly, I was dealing with the angst that Sonya and friends had been living though the past year. She showed me the photos. It was unbelievable. Forrest was a fifty-pound hairy mutt. Surely, I had just entered the Twilight Zone. To a trained eye—which I was—he looked more like a stocky Labrador-Shepherd mix that wiggled his round butt in typical bully fashion. While it was possible to imagine that his great uncle carried some bully genes, how did that make him a *dangerous* dog?

It didn't! Denver wanted any dog that looked like a pit bull destroyed. Period. It was a crime against the family dog—tearing families apart. It was a dangerous precedent that set off a chain reaction for copycat cities to follow. Soon after Denver, other fearful cities across the country would vote in favor of mindless breed bans. A plague that would kill thousands of innocent dogs and destroy our freedoms as Americans. Back to Forrest... Legal papers filed by Forrest's family helped to put the brakes on. As the drama started to drag on into the second month, everyone worried about the fate of Forrest. No one was allowed in for a visit—not even his grieving family. Given the inconceivable actions taken by Denver to enforce their crazy breed-ban thus far, we knew this dog's life was on the line. While Forrest was under the thumbs of Denver's canine Nazis, we were busy organizing into a team of avengers. Blowback on the authoritarian canine regime that had forever cast a black eye on the renegade city was past due. We had to stop them.

The group decided to organize a protest at the Denver Animal Shelter without a minute to waste. By this time, the bad news about Denver's deadly breed ban had spread far outside of the city limits. I would not be the only protester to arrive by plane. The former first wife of Richard Dreyfuss, Jeramie, had the longest flight. She was a colorful character, full of life and passion, who was now residing in Idaho. She was mad as hell and determined to get justice for Forrest, as was every soul that showed up that Saturday morning. We waved our signs, took pictures, and recorded video. We had plastered our pleas for the safe release of Forrest over social media sites and on our cameras when a few local TV stations eventually showed up. Every day we waited. Every day we worried. Weeks rolled by. The call came toward the end of a work day. Whatever was left to do would have to wait. Sonya was calling.

She sounded a bit out of breath this time, tipping me off that I was about to get important news. Her sentences came in rapid-fire succession as she finally blurted out a question: "Do you know anyone in California who would be willing to adopt Forrest?"

Before I could wrap my head around that question, she continued without pause. Here was the deal. The authorities had decided to play God and offer a compromise. Forrest would be released under one condition: He would go to an adopter living out of state, not to his family or any other Colorado resident. This person would need identification to verify a home address and sign an agreement never to return with the dog. And the clock was ticking; we only had seven days to get Forrest out.

Our fellow dog warrior David already knew the route to Denver. He had driven from California to attend our protest where he met Forrest's family—a family that had mushroomed into a small band of outraged activists. We would fight like it was our city. The horror was real to us. David hit the road again.

This trip, with the clock ticking, he made it there in record time. We knew Forrest was not safe until David sent us the word.

Three days later I got the call at daybreak. He called as soon as he had crossed state lines on Interstate 70. He had driven all night in route to California. Forrest was out of danger.

David was a true-blue hero to the real family Forrest was forced to leave behind. California would be Forrest's new home and he had lots of friends there waiting to meet him. We gathered and listened to David's ordeal with Denver authorities. No, it had not been as simple as writing a check for the release of their canine hostage. There were also documents that threatened legal action against David if he violated the agreement. All the while, we were watching tail-wagging Forrest, the "killer beast," bouncing around the room to greet us. No wonder his family had fought so hard to save his life. He would become big brother to David's other dog, a young, playful female of bully origins—both, Denver outlaws.

As I finish this chapter, more than ten years have passed. I can promise you that I did not get bored and morph into a fiction writer gone over to the dark side. It still feels like the Twilight Zone and I still have trouble believing it really happened. It still frightens me. Denver lost its mind. Family dogs lost their lives.

A crisis can spur anyone into action. Bearing witness to Denver rattled me to the core. It was a serious warning to dog owners everywhere. There are federal and state laws that impact the lives of millions. However, cities have their own mini-governments called "city councils." They set the agenda for city residents. They also make the rules that govern your everyday life. And this disaster was not going to happen in Brea, my city. Not on my watch. And I had my lucky charm standing at attention.

Janet helped organize our pro-active march to City Hall. The police department would not interfere as long as everyone walked in single file on sidewalks, careful not to obstruct pedestrian traffic. The Luv-a-Bully March was my shot across the bow. I would nip any talk of breed specific legislation in the bully bud. I had professional credentials and a small army of angry dog owners. We would be fierce opponents if there was even a whisper. There never was.

Denver residents had not been ready to battle an incompetent, reckless city council. I reached out to these council members several times to offer my testimony. Only one of them took my call. The others chose to remain deaf. This was a council that refused to look at facts and consult animal experts before unanimously voting to enact the ban. They chose their ignorant beliefs over their duty to responsibly govern. They forced brave, courageous, and law-abiding citizens to sacrifice their homes and communities. Those that could not flee sacrificed their dogs. Gryffindor and Forrest would win their battles. I have more stories to tell that I wish I did not.

This chapter is dedicated to all the brave warriors battling discrimination of any kind. Keep fighting.

Do you know what stuff is on the minds of *your* city council members?

Chapter Ten

Lucy

It's not the future you're afraid of. It's repeating the past that makes you anxious.
—Anonymous

I had secretly wanted a Scottish terrier, but it violated my principles to seek out breeders. The rescue mindset prevailed, and I made no secrets about it. In time, it became an unspoken rule to my staff: Adopt. So when a client had bred her Scottish terrier, and I knew the puppies were in an exam room waiting for me to bounce in, I tried to hide my enthusiasm. It didn't work, and before I knew it, I was offered a puppy. Six weeks later I brought Lucy home. We would enjoy seven wonderful years together before trouble started.

Something about Lucy was not right. First, I noticed her appetite was off. Ho-hum appetites often offer us the earliest clue. It's the one commonality that many illnesses share. So watch out for any changes in appetite. It's when you really need to start paying more attention.

Good doctors work in earnest like experienced puzzle-solvers—moving information around until everything fits. After talking with clients and asking lots of questions, we analyze the patient's history for relevant information. Next, our hands, eyes, and ears go to work. We make pertinent observations and record data. Sometimes, after just putting these two pieces together, we can look like a genius—puzzle solved. If not, we go back to gather more information. Next, we order routine lab work, like blood tests (CBC and chemistry panel) and a urinalysis, adding two more pieces of data, hoping to solve the puzzle. Looking at Lucy's lab reports only helped to rule out things like kidney or liver disease and blood cell abnormalities. Her symptoms remained an unsolved puzzle.

Next came the radiographs of her chest and abdomen. The first real clue was discovered—a suspicious shadow on her chest radiograph.

After my initial work-up, I consulted a veterinary radiologist. We discussed my dog like a typical patient—but there was nothing typical about how I was feeling. Dr. BK confirmed the abnormal density seen on the chest films. Without any more discussion, a biopsy of the suspect mass was recommended. I was unprepared for *that* news. It was all he needed to say for me to know that a tumor was first on his list of possibilities. Shit! I was rooting for an infection that I could kill with a silver bullet. That I understood "doctor talk" gave me an advantage as the owner of the patient, but it didn't mean that I would worry any less.

I held back the tears when I called Dr. CW, a talented surgeon with whom I had worked during my pre-vet years. I felt lucky that we had stayed friends. Opening the chest cavity to expose lung tissue required major surgery with its associated risks—putting me in the hot seat. As pet owners, we are called upon to make decisions for a life other than our own. Our pets are not burdened with serious decision-making. They are in the moment creatures without doubts or hesitation—which means they can't mess up like humans. Oh, the glory of being non-human!

To this day, I believe the surgeon was acting upon what he believed to be the best call. He removed the mass and sectioned off a part to peer at under the microscope. He reported the likelihood of it being a malignant tumor. I was devastated and pressed him hard. Was he sure? He would not commit. He was not a pathologist. Then, he threw another curve ball: "You know, if this is cancer and we wake up Lucy, she will be in a lot of pain." And without saying it, he did say it. If we woke Lucy up from anesthesia, she would die a painful death in the coming weeks or months. We shouldn't let her suffer.

I took a veterinary oath to prevent and provide the relief of animal suffering:

Being admitted to the profession of veterinary medicine, I solemnly swear to use my scientific knowledge and skills for the benefit of society through the protection of animal health and welfare, and the prevention and relief of animal suffering.

In an agonizing moment, I let Lucy go. That morning on the drive to the hospital, I had reassured Lucy that everything would be all right. I didn't feel guilty about saying those words because I was really talking to myself, as we know that's what humans do. But I did something else that was not predictable. I retrieved the entire mass and sent it out to a pathologist for examination. Of course, it would not matter for the patient, but it was the closure I personally needed. The report would no doubt confirm that I made the right choice. Except that it didn't.

Three days later I got the pathology report back. The diagnosis hit me hard. Neither the radiologist nor the surgeon had considered this possibility. Here's the lesson I would never forget: It's possible for the experts that advise us to get it wrong.

I became haunted by this question. Had I abdicated my own responsibility by handing over the reins to more experienced doctors? The answer was a harsh, "I guess so." In vet school, we are taught how to determine a differential diagnosis for each patient. That means, after doing a thorough patient workup, it's time to write down a list of every possible disease that could be matched to the patient's symptoms. Just keep looking (more tests, additional physical exams, get another doctor's opinion) until you find the last piece that solves the puzzle.

We scan our list of differential diagnoses, testing for each suspect illness, until the real criminal is found. Infectious causes, like an abscess, had been on my hopeful mind the very first time I looked at Lucy's X-ray. Why? Because infections have treatment plans unlike cancer. The shocking pathology report identified an infection of fungal origin, not a cancer. The pathologist nailed it. It was the final puzzle piece missed by me and my trusted colleagues. In the midst of my grief, anger was not far behind.

You won't find this cocktail in a bar. It's a mixture of grief and anger topped off with a heavy amount of guilt. It was toxic, and I drank it every day for years. Lucy's fungal disease could have been diagnosed with a simple blood test. But I and my esteemed colleagues had failed to make a complete textbook differential diagnosis list. So the test was never ordered.

One thing missing from Lucy's patient history were our frequent visits to Palm Springs for weekend getaways. Palm Springs makes up one of nine cities located in the Coachella Valley. Our second home condo was on a map of Southern California deserts—southeast from the San Bernardino Mountains to the northern shore of the Salton Sea. In general, residents of Southern California (more often the Central Valley) could encounter this soil organism just by breathing. Arid desert windstorms and construction sites are dust blowing machines. When the fungus gets an airlift, airborne spores can be inhaled. This was to be Lucy's fate.

Depending on geography, wherever you live or just visit, it's likely there are inherent health risks. Like mosquitoes and malaria in parts of Asia. Or heartworms in northern California. Keep in mind the places you've lived and visited. It's a relevant part of your and your pet's history. Respiratory symptoms (such as persistent cough or difficulty breathing accompanied by fatigue and possible fever) that do not respond to conventional therapies should raise an eyebrow for *Coccidioides immitis*—known as Valley Fever in humans.

For people and pets living in or visiting arid to semi-arid areas of the southwestern United States, this fungus should be on every doctor's differential list when persistent respiratory symptoms fail conventional treatments for suspected viral or bacterial infections. I was only partially right about what might be causing Lucy's symptoms. Yes, she had an infection. However, there are four classes of infectious agents: bacteria, viruses, fungi, and parasites. I had been stuck on only one of them—bacterial. The price of missing the correct diagnosis and losing a patient is every doctor's worst nightmare. By the end of that same year, my marriage had ended in divorce. I lost both my beloved Lucy and my best friend. It was the year from hell. I was a walking zombie.

Unlike the mind games played in vet school, this time I was tossed into a new bucket of suffering: dealing with the crisis of a wounded soul and self-doubt. I was given no date when l could expect to graduate from this double dose of grief and move on with life. In my zombie-like state, Mom helped me pack up and sell my house. Then strangely, I went to live with one of my sisters, something my rational mind would never do. Looking back, that move was an emotional "duck and run for cover." In the dog-less time zone that followed, I had no fur in my bed. I had no joy either. It would take another client with puppies to change all of that one year later.

Chapter Eleven

Rose

Grief never ends. But it changes. It's a passage, not a place to stay. Grief is not a sign of weakness, nor is it a lack of faith . . . it is the price of love.
—Unknown

It had been a full year of living with grief and regret when I first laid eyes on the pure white, wrinkled puppy. There were a total of nine pups waiting to be examined, one of them showing strange red blotches on the belly. I was pretty sure of the diagnosis, having seen it before. Puppy pyoderma (slang for a bacterial skin infection in puppies) was not uncommon. What was uncommon, even rare, was a solid white Boxer.

The cruel hard fact about pedigree breeders is their propensity to cull littermates with traits or deformities that don't pass the AKC muster. Solid white hair coats (along with white cats and other unrelated species) are known to carry the gene for deafness. Carrying the gene is not synonymous with actually being deaf. Some are, while others hear perfectly. More ethical breeders, like my client, will allow these less than privileged dogs to be adopted if they are sterilized to ensure they are never bred. Other breeder types feel justified to eliminate these "rejects" immediately. Life itself has no value to them—everything is about winning ribbons or making a profit. These heartless souls give me nightmares.

When I pulled the white puppy closer for examination, I made the fateful mistake of pausing to admire her face. Her facial folds of loose skin reminded me of a rose petal. Holding her vertically in suspension, I peered into her eyes; all the while she never squirmed. She just stared back at me. It was the first twinge of emotion I had felt toward a dog since those dark days of the past year. Caught completely off-guard, I hurried to write the prescription, wash my hands, and knock on the next exam door.

About two weeks later, I asked Janet to call about the puppy and make an explicit request. I wanted to see (more like visit) that puppy again. But that's not exactly what I told Janet. When the owner reported that the rash was gone, Janet pulled out her ace in the hole: "Doc just wants to be really sure. You know how she is. When is a good time for you to come in?"

I had thought a lot about wanting to see that puppy again. And Janet knew it. I felt something "in the moment" that day. I wasn't using my doctor brain to problem-solve. It was a happy feeling in my unhappy life. So, my heart was speaking, but having a difficult time. Memories of Lucy were still dishing out heaps of guilt and self-doubt, only less often. The uprooting winds of divorce and moving were still blowing, only not as heavy. Ending a marriage took its own toll of emptiness.

Can we love again while the clouds of grief are still lifting? Yes, we must always keep an open heart. Feelings of love are part of healing the soul. And I can prove it.

I still smile when I remember the first time I called the white puppy with wrinkles by name—"Rose." It would stick, especially since I had an Aunt Rose who I adored. I knocked on the door where Rose was waiting. After a little chit-chat with my client, I took the first step. A half-step, really. I wanted to confess my desire for Rose, but I just wasn't ready to commit. Being afraid and feeling unsure, I bargained for more time when I told a white lie. I had been on very friendly ground with a few of my clients, like Laura. Because Laura knew about my divorce, I told her I was still in the process of moving. So I asked her to keep the pup and let me visit. I don't know if she believed that story, but she agreed nonetheless. These pathetic visits went on for weeks.

The move into my sister's house had already happened, so there was no move-in date. There was no specific time when Rose would be coming home with me. It was a Sunday morning when I decided to take Rose for a car ride in a beautiful canyon not far from my sister's house. The calm pup was content to stay in the front seat next to mine the entire trip. As we drove along the winding road through a hillside shaded by trees, I started a conversation with my new passenger. I told Rose about Lucy and explained why I was so heartbroken. Minutes later, I had to pull off the road and park under a shady oak. Tears had started raining down my checks. Rose did it. She cracked the code. I held her and sobbed—full throttle.

After that Sunday afternoon car ride, Rose and I spent our first night together. I woke up happy knowing she was with me. That's when I knew I needed to have "the talk" with grieving pet owners. In my dog-less year, I was no better off. Things did not get any better. Protecting my heart from another loss was a lifeless existence. My life lesson taught me that pet lovers grieving a loss must keep that door open and never lock it.

Rose was my last non-rescue dog. Even though she was not breeder stock, I knew she was not going to end up at a shelter or in a box labeled free puppies in the parking lot of a grocery store. In other words, her life was not at-risk. In the next chapter I will tell you about Woody, the dog that forever changed me. Woody did end up in a box, as a pup that no one wanted. That's when I accepted the invitation to join the rescue community. I wanted to rescue more dogs like Woody.

Chapter Twelve

Woody

Fate is never fair. You are caught in a current much stronger than you are; struggle against it and you'll drown not just yourself but those who try to save you. Swim with it, and you'll survive.
—Cassandra Clare, *City of Ashes*

Woody had been dumped on the doorstep of Save A Pet, a non-profit rescue organization. Too young to be weaned from his mother, surrogate volunteers bottle fed him. Fast-forward ten years and, still, no one had adopted him. Being a shy, timid dog, Woody did not approach the front of his kennel to greet onlookers. As his kennelmates charged forward to rush the gate when visitors arrived, Woody stayed behind. An invisible, mid-sized, solid black mutt with a curved tail; some part Chow Chow, Shiba Inu, or perhaps Schipperke. In short, no one had ever seemed to notice he was there. Even I hadn't noticed him on the few times I visited. Had it not been for a deadly twist of fate, Woody was doomed to live out his life and die in that shelter. But that was not to be the end of his story. A nearly fatal dog attack sent us both to the hospital. Let me explain.

My weekend get-away spot was a little less than a two-hour drive from Orange County. On this particular weekend visit, I was traveling with my male cohort, arriving just around dusk. As he entered the front door to start unpacking, I stayed behind on the patio, soaking up the remaining warm sunset and staring out at the barren twenty-acre desert plot, littered with tumbleweeds that made it a humble refuge. The two old dilapidated barns that remained, long after the chickens were gone, added to its rustic charm. It was around 2001 when I began my weekend retreat to this Knott's Berry Farm-like property. It was noiseless and calming—everything missing from my busy city life. It was my ocean in the desert, an escape to find some serenity.

The cozy, one-bedroom farmhouse was built in the 1950s by an enterprising married couple to raise and sell chickens. Soon after I had purchased the vacant dilapidated property, an elderly neighbor from across the street stopped by to tell me about these two pioneers. After a few years of ranching, they had secured a contract with the famous Colonel Sanders. Kentucky Fried Chicken kept the chicken-ranching couple in business until the physical age of retirement forced them out of business. So it seemed fitting to call it The Ranch.

That weekend we had visitors. Woody and a few of his kennelmates from Save A Pet were being kept on the grounds at The Ranch to vacate kennel space for the Katrina refugees being flown in for housing and relocation. Tails were wagging and itching for some fun when I tossed a Frisbee into the air. All hell broke loose when one of the ranch dogs secured a choke hold on the shy newcomer, Woody, also en route to catch the Frisbee. Because I had agreed to provide temporary housing when asked, since there was a groundskeeper on the property, I was responsible for any outcome. It was an awful idea, far beyond a stupid one.

Without warning, Woody was suddenly down and held pinned to the ground by his neck. Unable to flee, Woody vocalized bone-chilling cries as he struggled to get away. My panicked screams for help traveled outside of earshot. A minute or two later, time was up. Woody's last minutes on earth were about to end in terrified and suffering pain. There were only seconds left to do something—anything! It was up to me to answer the 911 call. I could stay a helpless bystander or get into the fight.

In a complete act of desperation, I forcefully landed a swift kick to the attacker's chest. That blow was enough to loosen the killer's chokehold on Woody's throat, but not enough to protect him from another attack. Woody needed a bodyguard to get in front of the canine bullet until someone could respond to my screams for help. Before the unhinged dog could launch a second attack, I draped myself like a heavy blanket over Woody's torso. Fortunately, my adrenaline-fueled tight body grip worked as a shield until help finally came. I had yet to feel any pain. After I managed to drag Woody's bloody body into the house, I collapsed. As the second victim in the vicious mauling, I became the 911 call.

A deep, gaping neck wound had fully exposed Woody's jugular vein. You could see it pulse. With surgery, the wound eventually healed. Woody won his fight to live. That awful night would become Woody's "get out of jail free" card. He would never again return to shelter life. Obviously, I was a survivor, too. My surgical wounds eventually healed, but the trauma never faded. This wasn't some little skirmish over a Frisbee. An unknown killer lurked within the pack.

To this day, I am spooked by aggressive dog behavior. My rational mind knows that dangerous dog aggression is not common and human attacks are rare. Aggressive dogs asserting their dominance does not make them killers. What blows my mind is that the killer dog in this story, BW, was my dog by default. He had wandered onto my property as a stray—skinny and hungry—several years earlier. He had never shown any aggression toward my own dogs, and he was friendly with people. He had even slept in my own bed at The Ranch.

However, after the Woody incident, BW started to show aggression toward other dogs, too. Woody had somehow triggered his latent dog aggression. I have no explanation other than to recognize that there are human killers in our society, taking the lives of innocent people every day, putting all of us at risk. There is no "forgive and forget" for what they do. Whether or not to put down a dog proven to be dangerous is more of a responsibility than a decision. BW attacked the human shield—me. That he would have finished the job on Woody—I have no doubt in my mind. I could not live with that possibility again. So I paid the mental price. It was my responsibility. He would not live another day to harm another soul.

I was familiar with dog behavior that commonly played itself out with growling and threating postures. Early warning signs to back off were normal social dog etiquette. I had seen it many times. Learn to appreciate the growl. It's a warning. BW never growled.

Woody, already a greying senior dog, would live out the rest of his days with me—happy, loved and protected. Our shared ordeal fostered a unique bond between us. We adored each other for three more years. It still saddens me that we were robbed of the first ten, but the sweet memories live on.

Chapter Thirteen
People Food

There must be no barriers to freedom of inquiry. There is no place for dogma in science. The scientist is free, and must be free to ask any question, to doubt any assertion, to seek for any evidence, to correct any errors.
—J. Robert Oppenheimer

In vet school, the conventional wisdom bestowed upon students was the mantra that insisted that formulated pet food diets—anything certified by AAFCO (Association of American Feed Control Officials)—was the only way to go. This was reinforced by another seemingly popular belief that the public could not be trusted to prepare balanced meals for their pets. Cautionary tales about feeding "people food" to pets conjured up images of dogs binging on hot dogs and potato chips and cats eating only cans of StarKist tuna every day. Of course, this would be misguided and harmful over time. But it would take the toxicology class to wake me up.

Aflatoxin is a deadly toxin produced by the mold *Aspergillus flavus* that grows on peanuts and a few other crops, such as corn. Known to be a potent carcinogen, the U.S. Department of Agriculture (USDA) recognizes aflatoxin as a serious health risk. Moldy crops, discarded from human consumption, could and did find their way into the production of livestock feed, making cows and hogs sick. Purchased for next to nothing, these contaminated crops also found buyers in the pet food industry, making dogs and cats sick. The bottom line: Public health issues surrounding food are only human ones. The government doesn't give a damn about our pet companions. And neither does AAFCO.

At the root of the problem was AAFCO itself. For example, in their analysis, peanut hulls can be counted as fiber, and in doing so, they set the bar so low as to allow other inferior ingredients besides the hulls (like contaminated meats and meat byproducts) to be purchased by pet food manufactures. The result: Cheap inferior brands of pet food have flourished.

A pet food skeptic was born. And she never ate another peanut.

Starting in the 1960s, Science Diet was hailed as the pet food champion after proudly rolling out one prescription diet after another. This added testimony to an association between disease and diet. Later, I would come to see this nutritional advice more as a conflict of interest—less to do with science and more to do with sales. For the most part, it dominated nutritional training veterinarians received—which wasn't much. Sales reps for Science Diet were at every veterinary seminar and conference we attended. They often bought our lunches and dinners as they unloaded bags and cans for us to sample. And for a while, I bought into their hyped-up marketing campaigns—until I learned to read pet food labels and ask questions the reps didn't like. Your vet may not like your questions either.

It would be years later before I attempted to take on the pet food industry with an e-book, *How to Feed Your Dog—If You Flunked Rocket Science*. I wanted to expose the pitfalls of commercial diets and point fingers at giant corporations like Purina. My case against Purina (and other guilty pet food manufacturers) is how it defrauds pet owners. Case in point: Purina's fraudulent claims about Beneful being a naturally healthy diet cannot be proven. In fact, it's a bold-faced lie. The list of ingredients screams "Don't buy this one!" to informed shoppers who read pet food labels. To the uneducated, unsuspecting pet owner, clever advertising tricks and other gimmicks are sales tactics of manipulation. Cuts of red meat and colorful veggies plastered on shiny sacks of kibble is all part of the deception. It's a perfect storm when diets lacking any real nutritional value pass muster with AAFCO (a sell-out for big agriculture) to shake the hand of greedy corporate shareholders. All of it adds up to bigger profits—proof that thoughtless people are profitable. Just find the right advertising spin. But don't take my word for it; ask Google. Is pet food making pets sick?

The main objective of this book is to empower pet owners and shine light in dark places, the highlights of which point out important information. I want to steer you away from the dogma with knowledge that can be a turning point for your pet's benefit. Roads that sometimes point in opposite directions. Signs that say *This Way to Better Health and Fewer Problems*. Nothing will have a greater impact on the health and wellbeing of animals, including the human model, than what is chewed and swallowed. Diet is the universal starting point.

Fortunately, this news flash came early in my life. I was sick and overweight as a teenager and well into my twenties. I battled infection after infection. My bouts of illness included pneumonia, hepatitis, recurrent strep throat and bladder infections. The bugs that really liked me then won't find the same welcome mat today. My rehabilitation started when I stopped drinking sodas and gave up the donut shop. Slowly, I became a vegetable lover and stopped eating fast food, too. I never had to diet to lose my teenage fat—I just ate differently. I got healthy, too. Sadly, our domestic pets don't have a choice—they depend on us. We are their hunters.

On a sliding scale, non-human grade commercial pet foods simply range from bad to not as bad. In more recent years, progressive and ethically minded pet food companies have jumped on the pure meat and organ bandwagon. Not parts of the chicken—the whole bird. Zero carbohydrates. Contrast that with standard commercial diets containing less than 30 percent protein and carbohydrates as high 40 percent. Using only 100 percent human grade ingredients, the ancestral based diets are not heat-treated dehydrated balls of kibble. They are frozen or air-dried, making the food more digestible and nutrient rich. Yes, you will pay more not to feed cheap, low quality and possibly dangerous pet foods. But all bets are on that your pet will be passing annual physical exams with flying colors. My dogs do.

Chapter Fourteen

The Dogie Bag

Curmudgeons speak up because they have to, because it's become critically important for them to tell the truth as they see it. Telling the truth is as natural to them once more as it was when they were children. The fact that no one cares to listen is inconsequential. Curmudgeons speak up, raise their voices, stand for something too right to be silent about anymore, whatever the cost, despite a world that deals with what it doesn't want to hear by crucifying the messenger.

Increasingly these days, they're being called by another name: whistleblower.
—Lionel Fisher

It was sometime in the year 2000 when I discovered a newly published book by Donald R. Strombeck, DVM, PhD—my favorite professor at UC Davis. I never had an innate interest in the rather gross subject of gastroenterology. Not really. It was how this particular professor presented the subject material, making it both interesting and practical. I actually looked forward to his lectures and came to loath all others who expected rote memorization. His lectures turned vomiting and diarrhea into challenging mysteries to be solved. As he presented us with different patient scenarios—describing the history and symptoms followed by laboratory results to study—Strombeck was teaching us how to diagnosis and prescribe treatments in the real world. He set the stage and we performed well, or failed, like real doctors. Because many of our patients fall into the GI category—complaints of poor appetites, weight loss, vomiting and diarrhea of unknown causes—it was critical to master the subject material. I kept his notes for many years. Surprisingly, his newest book was not another medical textbook. I was curious to locate it and excited to read the title: *Home-Prepared Dog and Cat Diets: The Healthful Alternative.* He let the cat (and the dog) out of the bag.

Fourteen years after he had helped graduate the Class of 1986, he blew the whistle on the pet food industry. In a November 2008 interview, he had this to say when asked about the pet food industry:

> *It has become a gigantic, multibillion-dollar industry. The industry learned to advertise and describe their products as being the "best," at least according to them. But they have tried to control the education of veterinarians on pet nutrition. They send a lot of literature and books to veterinarians who teach. One of the dogmas they have promoted, and that many veterinarians have bought into, is that you should only feed commercial pet foods because they are balanced and provide everything an animal needs. And that you shouldn't feed any human food or add any table scraps to it. So, if you go to most veterinarians, that is what they are going to tell you. Most of the money available for research on small-animal nutrition comes from the industry as well. It is a conflict of interest.*

> AAFCO is a mutual admiration society representing the pet food industry. They are from the industry. They say that they can police themselves and don't need any government interference. And that's the way it operates. There haven't been any changes there, and so the only thing that will cause them to change the way they do things is if they lose a lot of money from scares like pet food recalls.

It would be an honor for me to pin an award on my esteemed university professor for telling the public the gritty truth. To the readers of his book, Strombeck had this to say:

> Pet foods are not always nutritionally complete and balanced. Problems develop because of nutrient deficiency or excess. Thereby, diets and eating habits can contribute to medical problems and reduced life expectancy.

Here was his reprimand delivered to the pet food industry:

> Pets are breaking down from disease at an unprecedented rate from a variety of problems. Why are so many pets getting cancers, renal failure, hepatic diseases, multitudes of skin and coat problems? Diseases and illnesses we simply should not be seeing. Illnesses and poor nutrition affect each other.

It was all the validation I needed to satisfy my growing skepticism. After reading it cover to cover, eager clients took home recipes on photocopied pages. Their enthusiasm signaled the time was ripe for a sea change. Pet owners had finally been given permission and Strombeck's blessing. It was more than okay to feed pets people food—it was far better. There was no higher authority to challenge this edict. The begging canine furball had been right all along. Dogs are true carnivores by nature; they thrive on meat and animal fat. Our pet carnivores (cats and dogs) have no nutritional need for carbohydrates. None. There is only one reason carbs are so heavily used in typical commercial diets: money.

Inspired by Strombeck's collection of easy-to-cook recipes and the impressive number of positive responses by my patients, I was hooked. I called this new venture "The Dogie Bag." I did not inherit the cooking gene, but the idea of mixing together ground turkey meat, eggs (plus dried egg shells for calcium), and broccoli seemed simple enough. I scooped the concoction into mini-bread pans and popped them into the oven. The smell made me hungry enough to eat the loaves myself. So I often cheated and did take a bite. Meaty Muttloaf, as I would call the first item on the Dogie Bag menu, was a hit!

Next came the delivery of a glass door freezer in my hospital lobby for display. About one year later, I crowned myself *Royal Dog Chef* and leased space in a Palm Springs shopping mall to open a commercial kitchen and cook even more meatloaves. I was a three-day weekend warrior dog chef, commuting back to Orange County to resume my other life—the veterinarian.

This double life lasted about two years before it was time to hang up the apron. The expenses and debts of this new part-time enterprise became an accounting disaster. Numbers do not lie, and I was exhausted. My entrepreneurial spirit had overlooked the need for key partnerships and better planning. Hindsight is a bitch.

Soon, other dog chefs started popping up everywhere with their own versions of home-cooked meals. I watched a trend become a full-fledged movement. If you are ready to don your dog chef apron, be sure to follow nutritionally complete pet food recipes. BalanceIT.com and The Whole Dog Journal are good places to start. Or consult the Daily Canine Diet Guidelines Food Chart with its corresponding Food Calculator (see Appendix 1).

Grocery shopping can be cost-effective (especially when using eggs as a protein source) and as a bonus, your pet will never fall victim to future pet food recalls. Later, I would graduate to embrace raw pet food diets. This took a little more convincing. Feeding raw food (meat, organs and bone) is going one big step further. Do your homework first. Consult PetFoodAdvisor.com for the better brands to buy, or study the works of Australian veterinarian Dr. Ian Billinghurst, father of the BARF diet (Biologically Appropriate Raw Food).

Sidestepping the pet food industry with cooked or raw food diets is the single most important decision pet owners will ever make. Make the investment. The return on your money will guarantee your pet's optimum health and well-being. Illness is a heavy price to pay.

Food is the best veterinary insurance policy you can buy.

Chapter Fifteen

Lola

If we stay in one place, we will become outdated.
—Satoru Iwata

I first examined the snowy white Bichon Frise-poodle mix soon after a polite older couple had adopted her, making it abundantly clear that they adored their new little bundle of joy. The young Lola passed her routine physical exam with flying colors before receiving the rabies vaccine her owners requested. The couple of two had become a family of three. I was sure Lola would provide them with many happy years to enjoy her companionship. So, why had they returned as my first 9:00 a.m. appointment ten days later? I proceeded with caution knowing that unexpected surprises rarely came with good news. I was right.

It was the true test of the number one rule: No pet could be dropped off, or scheduled for euthanasia, without first securing the doctor's permission. They did not have my permission, nor would they receive it that morning. After our last visit, Lola had sent them into a panic. The couple had witnessed several seizure episodes, but never called to report this. I could see how upset they were, so I skipped the "Why didn't you call me?" question. Somehow, their thinking had catapulted them to reach a fatal conclusion: The need to end Lola's life that morning in my office. Now I too was upset. As I watched Lola bounce around the exam room, I had only one question: What was the Kool-Aid they were drinking? First, I had to understand.

Their fatal conclusion rested upon twisted thinking and emotion, not on any facts or logic. It was a toxic stew of self-doubt and failure to comprehend what might be really happing with Lola. I was quickly running through my list of differentials, looking for the best possible scenario I could present. As a young (less than three years of age) and otherwise healthy dog, Lola could be experiencing her first bouts of seizure activity as an epileptic pup. Patients are generally pronounced "epileptic" when no other cause for seizures can be found. It's pretty much what we call a rule-out diagnosis. When you can't determine the seizure cause in a young dog (considered under three years of age) with no other symptoms of disease, you can bet you've got an epileptic on your hands. Normally, the doctor's job is to reassure the family that this disorder is likely to be well-controlled with medication; in medical jargon, a good prognosis or favorable outcome. Treatable conditions that can be restored to a good quality of life are basically received as good news. However, after picking the brains of this older, anxious couple, nothing less than a total cure was going to change their minds. I had never encountered such a dire situation. From Lola's recent medical history, I grasped for a straw—the rabies vaccine.

In the most calm and reassuring voice I could muster, I pointed to the possibility of the rabies vaccine. It was more hope than reason allowed. However, vaccines don't get the blame often enough for kicking off a cascade of autoimmune reactions, not to mention cancers at the injection site. Cautiously, I dumped all of Lola's eggs into the vaccine basket.

Of course, vaccines have also prevented deadly infectious diseases in canines and other species. Besides rabies, dogs are notably protected against distemper and parvoviruses. The story of Lola kicks off the debate on vaccines in the adult (over one year) companion pet population (a story to be continued).

Back in the exam room, I sold the owners on the possibility of a vaccine reaction. I judged some relief by the couple's expression as I talked. They listened, but they were unwilling to risk another disturbing eyewitness episode of a seizuring Lola. I had to buy my precarious patient some time. Reluctantly, the couple agreed to leave her with me. After they left, I made a beeline phone call to Dr. Jean Dodds, an expert on vaccinosis (any number of adverse reactions that occur post-vaccination). She more than believed my rabies shot hunch. Dodds drew a bullseye target on it. I started Lola on her recommended treatment protocol as soon as we hung up the phone. Lola had just dodged a deadly bullet—a totally uncalled for death.

Seven days later, I called the owners. Lola was responding and had not had another seizure. The frail couple returned to visit her. I explained that while I could not guarantee that Lola would never have another seizure, it was at least possible she would not. The reunion was so emotional that I stepped out of the room before I let heavy tears of gratitude fall. I have spent my entire career living for moments like this one. It's the hard-fought success stories that help balance out the failures. A sort of counterbalance against the line-up of medical casualties that make some days feel like a M*A*S*H unit. I needed hope to stay in the game. Lola, and other success stories like hers, gave me that hope and more.

We slowly tapered the steroids over several months. Lola never had another seizure. I made sure Lola's medical record reflected the solid proof needed when I wrote her Letter of Exemption.1 In that letter, I firmly stated that any future vaccination with the rabies vaccine could prove to be life-threatening. Ironically, it was.

During the time I was in practice, my blog, *Dog-Breath*, took stabs at controversial hot topics like pet foods, vaccines, and other mainstream veterinary debates. I was an outspoken critic on subjects that seemed determined to remain buried in the status quo, such as yearly routine vaccinations. Vaccine postcards had become commonplace scare tactics to fill up appointment slots—easy money that had nothing to do with whether or not the vaccines were justified. Annual vaccines were also promoted by Big Pharma sales reps who printed out the reminder postcards and handed them out to us like free candy on Halloween. All the while, a trusting and naive pet-owning public remained dutiful. It was dirty pool and I had a real problem with it. It would take another big shake-up, like Strombeck's book, for me to join ranks. This time the American Animal Hospital Association provided the ammunition needed and I was itching for the fight. *How to Protect Your Pet from a Vaccine Junkie* was a blogpost-turned-eBook. Here's why.

In 2011 the American Animal Hospital Association (AAHA) concluded a three-year vaccine task force study and published their findings. It was an honest attempt to cut through the "science" of vaccine marketing jargon and get to the real heart of the matter. Experts from the fields of immunology, infectious diseases and other researchers teamed up to publish their unbiased findings. While the holistic veterinary community embraced the sensibility of these new guidelines, others did not. To our dismay, it was only a guideline written for doctors, not a public mandate. The sweeping change in vaccine protocols, which was desperately warranted, did not have a single muscle of enforcement.

Although the public could access the AAHA document online, it was not user friendly for lay people to understand or interpret. Hence, my motivation to digest its content for public regurgitation. *How to Protect Your Pet from a Vaccine Junkie* was written as a playbook for pet owners, a weapon against the almighty veterinarian not willing to give up bread-and-butter vaccines. So pet owners must be able to, first of all, scrutinize which vaccines are necessary (the core vaccines2) and, secondly, question the need for pets past one year of age to receive repeated vaccines. Keep in mind, the typical house pet has little to no exposure to these viruses, unlike dogs and cats kept at animal shelters or by unscrupulous breeders. In other words, your pet's lifestyle and possibly where you live should determine the legitimate level of risk for infectious disease. Not all veterinarians take this common-sense approach to vaccination. You should.

In recent years, concerns about over-vaccination have been met with an option to perform *titer testing*. Here's how that works. Vaccines stimulate the immune system to make specific proteins called *antibodies*. Antibodies are like programmed missiles that target a specific virus or bacteria. These antibodies are measured by titer testing a sample of blood to determine if your pet is protected against specific diseases in past vaccines given. Blood samples can be measured fourteen days post-vaccination to determine the immune response. The ability to positively test for these antibodies negates the need for re-vaccination. It's good science and best standard of care. Unfortunately, and without merit, the AAHA's 2011 guidelines conservatively issued a three-year interval for the core vaccines.

Although it was a step in the right direction, away from the automatic pilot of yearly vaccination, it failed to address concerns about blindly repeating vaccines at preconceived intervals. In fact, repeated titer testing has shown protective antibodies lasting up to seven years or longer after a single adult vaccine given at twelve months of age. This arbitrary three-year interval has drawn sharp criticism from Dr. Ron Schultz, Professor and Chair of the Department of Pathobiological Sciences at the School of Veterinary Medicine at the University of Wisconsin-Madison. Dr. Schultz is considered to be one of the foremost experts on immunology and vaccinations for pets. Back in 1992 (twenty-six years ago as of 2018), Schultz wrote this statement in the medical textbook, *Current Veterinary Therapy*, volume XI:

> *A practice that was started many years ago and that lacks scientific validity or verification is annual revaccination. Almost without exception there is no immunologic requirement for annual revaccination. Immunity to viruses persists for years in the life of the animal.*

Many have judged AAHA's three-year protocol as a mere appeasement to its membership—practicing veterinarians and its ties to Big Pharma. In other words, don't bite the hand that feeds you. I'm going to let Dr. Schultz have the last word:

> *Vaccines for diseases like distemper and canine parvo-virus, once administered to adult animals, provide lifetime immunity. Profits are what vaccine critics believe is at the root of the profession's resistance to update its protocols. Without the lure of vaccines, clients might be less inclined to make yearly*

veterinary visits. Vaccines add up to 14 percent of the average practice's income, and veterinarians stand to lose big.

It's time to blow the whistle on any veterinary medical practice unwilling to adapt to the prevailing scientific literature on vaccination. In my veterinary evolution, hospital staff mailed out reminders for annual wellness exams, not vaccines. In our wellness plans, vaccines were given *only* if deemed necessary and at no extra cost. Our focus stressed the importance of annual physical exams, finding problems sooner rather than later. We talked about diet, measured and recorded weights, checked dental hygiene, and recommended natural supplements and other preventative health measures. Dog owners were offered vaccine titers in lieu of the DHP vaccine.

I told the truth. I got out of the vaccine business. I did just fine. And oh, by the way, my own dogs were never vaccinated again after their one-year birthdays. Like me, they spent all day in a hospital environment. None of them caught any infectious diseases, not even the kennel cough bug—for which they were never vaccinated. Now, for the rabies saga.

Sometime in the 1940s, rabies became and remains the only state-mandated pet vaccine. Whether you and your dog are fenced-in city dwellers or if your home is a place that sprouts a backyard of attractive food items and shelter for wildlife creatures such as bats, raccoons, foxes and coyotes—this is not a consideration. It also doesn't matter if your dog is a sixteen-year-old toothless Chihuahua. Rabies certificates are the law of the land. Animal Control, boarding services and grooming facilities and maybe even your own vet can play that card. In this "one size fits all" certification, nothing else matters. But it does matter, and it matters a lot to pet lovers worried about the risk of side effects.

Any risk-benefit ratio attempts to measure the level of risk before taking some particular action against its potential benefits. Basically, a certain level of risk must be accepted as necessary to achieve the benefits. Consider the benefits of owning a car to secure a job. The benefit of employment far exceeds the risk of an auto accident. That's a no-brainer. But when we allow thoughtless laws to dictate how we vaccinate our pets, at some point the benefit will equal zero. That's when risk is unacceptable.

Canine rabies vaccines were state-mandated when there was potential human health risk—the possibility of encountering a rabid dog. Protecting the family dog was in line with protecting humans. It was never about the dog, per se. Over decades, urban sprawl has pretty much segregated the house dog away from dangerous encounters with wildlife. Our lifestyles have changed, but not laws dating back to seventy years ago. Beyond wasted veterinary dollars is the risk of multiple rabies vaccines over the lifetime of your pet. Every vaccine carries health risks – similar to a game of Russian roulette.

We need pet owners to support The Rabies Challenge Fund:

The Rabies Challenge Fund has been working for a decade to extend the legally required interval for rabies vaccinations to five and then seven years, in an effort to reduce the number of unnecessary vaccinations our dogs would be required to have over their lifetimes. The Rabies Challenge Fund Charitable Trust will determine the duration of immunity conveyed by rabies vaccines. The goal is to extend the required interval for rabies boosters to 5 and then to 7 years. This project depends primarily upon grassroots gifts for funding the costs of conducting the requisite vaccine trials.

> *Our contributions to date have come mostly from kennel clubs and private individuals. (See rabieschallengefund.org)*

Two-year-old Lola developed a seizure disorder that might have gone undiagnosed as epilepsy. Most adverse vaccine reactions are not immediate; many, like hives, can show up hours later. Like Lola's case, most autoimmune triggered disease and associated cancers won't rear ugly heads for weeks or months. As time passes, it gets more difficult to pin the tail on the vaccine donkey. Just remember this donkey is real.

Something to ponder: Following the logic of pet vaccine schedules, after our kids receive a multitude of childhood vaccines, why are they not vaccinated again when they are teenagers and then again as adults, repeating the same vaccine cocktails? I'm going to let Dr. Shultz say it one more time:

> *Vaccines for diseases like distemper and canine parvo-virus, once administered to adult animals, provide lifetime immunity. Profits are what vaccine critics believe is at the root of the profession's resistance to update its protocols. Without the lure of vaccines, clients might be less inclined to make yearly veterinary visits. Vaccines add up to 14 percent of the average practice's income, and veterinarians stand to lose big.*

NOTES

1. Eighteen states have rabies medical exemptions: Alabama, California, Colorado, Connecticut, Florida, Illinois, Maine, Massachusetts, Maryland, New Hampshire, New Jersey, Nevada, New York, Oregon, Pennsylvania, Vermont, Virginia, Wisconsin
2. **Core vaccines:**
   Dogs: Distemper, Hepatitis, Parvo (all in one combo: DHP vaccine) and Rabies.
   Cats: Feline Viral Rhinotracheitis, Calcivirus, Panleu-kopenia (all-in-one combo: FVRCP vaccine) and Rabies.

Chapter Sixteen

Brad Pit

Opinion is the medium between knowledge and ignorance.
—Plato

If I had to guess, the rescued dog was a fifty-fifty split—half beagle and the other half spilling into the murky "pit bull" waters. And I'd probably be right. The kind stranger who took him off the streets named him Brad Pit. He was a handsome boy, so the name proved quite fitting. However, when I first laid eyes on him, he was a very sick dog that would reveal his Prince Charming side later. In fact, he was a pitiful mess (pun intended). As a favor to a friend, I drove out to see him. I had been told that the antibiotic was not working. Not an uncommon problem. Maybe I would just need to switch up his meds. So I was shocked to see a hairless dog that looked more like the shell of a lobster. He had a patchy red glow as if his fur had been seared off to expose raw skin. Both ear canals were swollen shut and oozing purulent material (fancy name for puss). He looked to be in such pain, I thought he might try to bite as I approached. But all this smelly dog did was wag his tail when I looked at him. It was a jaw-dropping, teary-eyed moment.

I had to convince the well-meaning but clueless rescuer to let me treat Brad at my hospital. So I made an offer he could not refuse: all veterinary care at no cost. It was literally a matter of life or death for the dog (I think he may have suspected as much). Brad's treatments would become an intense two-month rehabilitation. Fortunately, I had enlisted the help of my dedicated staff. Weeks of daily skin care included soaks with medicated shampoos, ear flushes, and multiple antibiotics to fight the infection. Although Brad showed modest improvement, he was not making the real progress I had expected. What puzzle piece was I missing? On occasion, I refer patients to a nearby top-notch veterinary dermatologist. This time I referred my rescue dog, Brad. It was our second car trip together. As I drove, my smarty-pants inner veterinarian reduced herself to humble doctor status. On the bright side, I'm always an eager student. The experience would make me a better doctor. And it surely did.

Dr. WR nailed it on the history and visual exam. I was about to get my first crack at treating a flesh-crawling bacterium that I had only read about—a deadly bacterium called MRSA: *Methicillin-resistant Staphylococcus aureus*. The typical (and easily treated) staph skin infection had morphed into an atypical new smart bug. MRSA is a virulent bacterial strain that renders many of the antibiotics commonly used against it useless. When MRSA spreads from the skin to invade vital organs, the patient's life starts ticking on a medical stopwatch. In a race against time, the search is on to find a bigger, more powerful gunslinger. This devilish germ makes headline news, claiming its human casualties.

The frightening possibility that our professors had warned us about in pharmacology class, MRSA was the real-life prediction coming true—the hatching of super bugs. We understood that what sounded like science fiction was not, although none of us wanted to believe it. We were warned that the continued indiscriminate use of antibiotic wonder drugs was a breeding ground for antibiotic resistors. The message was clear: Antibiotics had unintended consequences. These powerful drugs should never be used until there is a reasonable diagnosis. Don't treat symptoms. Don't be *that* doctor.

Bacteria live on an evolutionary fast track, so germs that survive treatment with one antibiotic soon learn to resist others. Once upon a time, common infections caused by *Staphylococcus aureus* were wiped out with good, old-fashioned penicillin. Not anymore. The heartbeat of evolution goes on to insure enhanced survival. So when microscopic single-celled organisms were gifted with genetic resistance, a bacterial Frankenstein was unleashed.

Methicillin is a semisynthetic form of penicillin. Our love affair with penicillin dates back to the 1940s. Its discovery led to magic-bullet treatments that battled a wide range of infections, helping doctors to save countless lives. Forty years after the penicillin era began, our professor's stern warnings about doctors writing lazy prescriptions was the harbinger of a medical disaster. Now we keep chasing super bugs with more sophisticated and costly antibiotics. Modern medicine has entered a new war against microbes, an enemy so small they cannot be detected with the naked eye. Its irrelevant size says nothing of its power to kill. Brad was on a bacterial hit list.

Three days later, a skin culture confirmed WR's diagnosis. Resistant bacteria had invaded Brad's deeper layer of skin tissues. His culture was positive for MRSA. Puzzle solved. Second opinions can be lifesaving. A second opinion saved Brad Pit. Before his treatment ended,

I would fall in love again. This time with a Denver outlaw that greeted everyone with a tail wag and loved to lick my toes. It's people who scare me, not dogs.

Part Three
New Beginnings

Chapter Seventeen

Going Broke

*You learn more from losing than winning.
You learn how to keep going.*
—Morgan Wootten

I've never been fond of the word *retirement*—"to withdraw, to go away, to retreat." My definition was the total opposite. In my world, I would be doing a lot more of what I wanted to do and a lot less of what I didn't. There was no rocking chair waiting for me, not even a date the chair would be delivered. It was the collapse of financial markets and the housing industry in years 2008 and 2009 that gave me the big boot. Stories my grandparents told about The Great Depression echoed in my thoughts. Fear was in the air and it was real. Over the following years, I witnessed friends and clients losing jobs and houses. As incomes dried up and Wall Street raped retirement accounts, any thought about the future felt like a panic attack. After the panic wore off, a true-blue depression followed.

Two years into the financial crisis, I had a decision to make. Hospital revenues had not rebounded, and surpluses had dried up. The monthly payroll was breaking the camel's back. I could no longer afford to pay myself and my associate veterinarian. One of us had to go. I could not hang on any longer.

So, I packed another U-Haul truck and said my goodbyes. My weekend love affair with the Sonoran Desert was about to become a full-time relationship.

I scraped up enough money to buy an old dilapidated hotel in Desert Hot Springs—vintage 1957. (Curiously, I was only three years old when they had broken ground.) Looking North from the I-10 Freeway, Desert Hot Springs shared breathtaking mountain views and windmill terrain with its sister city, Palm Springs. While both cities are connected by two main roadways, Indian Canyon and Gene Autry Trail, they are widely separated by the price of dirt. I would be living in the poorer city.

It seemed logical to buy the deserted roadside hotel. My veterinary career had been suspended and my meager IRA had been reduced to the purchase of a nice car. The hotel would be a bunker for me and close friends in distress. The five-thousand-square-foot property had eight bedrooms, each with a private bath and shared café kitchenette. The main building had all the characteristics of a small house—like an owner's unit. It featured a full-sized kitchen and living room that spilled out to the pool courtyard. Another private bedroom and bath—complete with a laundry room and office. It bore all the earmarks of a living/working environment. However, when I bought the place, I saw a spacious commune, something I had never even considered before. But these were not normal times. I was navigating a financial meltdown.

By New Year's Day 2011, things were not getting much better, except that none of my at-risk friends had needed a place to crash. Considering that I was not living bunker style and still had a cash reserve from the sale of my veterinary practice, I'd put my plan B to work. I finished all the hotel rehab projects, put up a website, filed an LLC and opened for business.

Less than a year later, the welcome mat was out. It was a red-carpet invitation to dog-lovers everywhere. The marketing plan was simple; the message clear. At the Dog Spa Resort and Wellness Center, LLC, our doors opened to dog paws of any size or breed. No pet restrictions and no pet fees. Family dogs were treated like kids on vacation. The paws had free roam, without leashes, to hang out. Social dogs lounged poolside with their owners and played in our dog park. It was the canine version of a Disneyland. As intended, I created the exact opposite atmosphere of a veterinary hospital. No weird smells or scary sounds. It was time to have some fun with the dogs and their owners. A personal lifestyle makeover. I really thought I had retired from practice. It was fun for a while.

The business tagline boasted, "All dogs vacation here free!" It was my shout-out to dog lovers everywhere. I wanted a special place just for them and the family dog, of course. I got more than I bargained for. I got trouble.

The first time I thought it was just a fluke. A guy at the front gate with a dog he wanted groomed. When I tried to explain that he was at a hotel, not a grooming shop, he looked away and pointed to the signage on the building. "It says you are a dog spa," he argued. "Sorry, sir, but this is only a hotel that is dog friendly."

Unsatisfied, he left. And when these people didn't randomly show up, they called to make appointments. People also asked if we boarded dogs. When unwanted grooming catalogs started landing in our mailbox, it was time to investigate. A Google search found us popping up on Internet sites with listings for pet groomers. Our bingo moment had unearthed an infestation by Internet spiders crawling our website. Translation by these creepy crawlers lumped us into the pet grooming universe.

Never understate the powerful persuasion of a name. Take note future business owners.

Next came an ugly realization: the very word *dog* also caught the attention of people looking to dump theirs in the hopes that our building offered some kind of dog business. Desperate people came knocking. A single mom was moving and could not take the family dog. I saw her kid waiting in the front seat of a beat-up car and that was the last time the kid saw his dog. Fortunately, the pup was small, young and cute. It was only a matter of hours until one of my Facebook friends saw the posting and replied. That pup went on to live a better life.

Another uninvited guest at the gate was holding a puppy and asking if I had lost one. Of course, I had not lost a puppy—who does that? Instinctively, I opened the gate to get more information. Before I could say no, he launched the pup safely through the opening and ran off. That skinny flea infested filthy pup also went on to live a much better life. I didn't have to wonder why rescue groups were always busting at the seams. There was too much supply of unwanted pets and not enough demand—my favorite rant to follow.

Living in a poor town is rich fertilizer for compassionate hearts. So I picked up all the strays I could catch. Somedays I felt like a dog rescue person. Hell, I was one of those nuts too, but I was living in a hotel, not an animal sanctuary.

Now for my rant:

No more shopping for puppies! Get over your breed obsession. Dial it down to preferences and adopt. Shelters and non-profit rescue organizations need community support to protect innocent lives. Run of the mill animal

shelters are nothing more than a prison trap. When nobody comes for the unwanted dog or cat, it's a death sentence. Give your money to a breeder, and another animal dies.

End of rant.

A few years down the road, I surrendered my genius idea for the quirky title, The Dog Spa Resort and Wellness Center. It was time to admit the problematic nature of a name. The sign came down and another went up. At the Desert Hot Springs Inn, the unwanted calls and visits eventually stopped, but not those damn grooming catalogs.

Chapter Eighteen

Sabbatical

The two most important days in your life are the day you are born, and the day you find out why.
—Mark Twain

While I had enjoyed the creative aspects of the hotel remodel and marketing, I quickly learned that I was not cut out to be an innkeeper. Less than a year later, I concluded that innkeeping sucked. Making coffee, washing dirty (sometimes gross) laundry, and delivering extra rolls of toilet paper to complete strangers was a dead-end job that felt like quicksand. I began to struggle with a mini identity crisis of my own doing. I was not that old fart, retired vet, pursuing her lifelong passion to be a bed and breakfast hostess—although that lovely creature probably does exist somewhere on the planet. Helping animals was my passion—a passion that had succumbed to an undiagnosed case of burnout. James Harriot's ghost began to haunt me.

It was the same three words every time: *It's not noble.* Not a voice, more like a tap on the shoulder. *Hey, what you are doing—it's not noble.* It made me feel bad. I finally realized that my hotel identity had squashed out the last thirty-five years of my life. My first clue came in how I introduced myself. To everyone in my retirement life, I was the adventurous owner and creator of the Dog Spa Resort. And I had lots of interesting stories to share.

So the DVM just disappeared from my name. I owned the ultra-dog friendly hotel in Desert Hot Springs—the first of its kind. When my past veterinary career leaked out (and it often did), it was a green light for pet owners to start probing me with questions. Ugh. I quickly retorted and emphasized "retired" veterinarian. I had to mute the conversation for safety reasons. I simply disagree with standard veterinary protocols—a one-size-fits-all approach—on pet foods and vaccination schedules. News that the prescription pet food they are feeding their pets—often recommended by their own vet—is worthless. This was the last thing they wanted to hear. When I screeched about annual vaccine reminders, it made them doubt the veterinary care their pets were receiving. It was a no-win situation. I was the proverbial captain without a ship. So I dived deep and went underground. Until Harriot's shoulder tap became ever more annoying.

I'll follow that confession with another. I'm a bookaholic reader of non-fiction, heavy into personal biographies along with health and science topics. As the shoulder-tapping continued, I found myself in a real funk. It was time to look for answers. My quests usually begin with my nose in a book or a lunch date conversation with a close friend. I don't exactly remember the question Brad had asked, only the intense feeling as I responded. As I recalled a recent visit to the local animal shelter (per invitation by my sister Sandy who had landed her post-retirement dream job as an adoption counselor) I was hit with waves of emotion. After introducing me to her co-workers as her sister the vet, I felt myself reaching for my medical black bag—tossed in the lost and found bin seven years ago. I felt empty. I needed to matter again. It was *noble* to matter.

To "kill two birds with one stone" is a metaphor I am particularly fond of. It speaks to a kind of problem-solving efficiency. And I had two problems. First, my life as a zookeeper (intended pun) was a joke. It was an endless source of problems, dealing with reservations and guests and anything else that could go wrong. Second, my stint in the hotel business proved to be one big fat money pit. After five years, profit and loss statements were still red ink sheets of paper. Profits were being gobbled up by frequent repair bills, insurance policies, property taxes, health department inspectors, and hot summer vacancies. Debt was piling up. In my sixth decade of life, I had to wake up to the fact that I had maxed out my credit cards to pay business expenses and personal bills. Bottom line: I was working without a paycheck.

I thought only reckless people who blew money on expensive cars, fancy clothes and exotic vacations racked up credit card debt. The "me" in the age of retirement had bought a used Subaru, shopped at discount stores like TJ Maxx (my favorite), and vacations were fond memories. I had gambled a small fortune to buy and rehab a 1957 hotel only to learn that there is a serious ebb and flow problem in the seasonal vacation rental business. I had too much ebb. It was time to face some very unpleasant music. I needed to create flow. And the flow needed to matter. First, I fired the innkeeper—me.

In my heart of hearts, I had planned to volunteer my veterinary skills to help non-profit rescue groups in my golden years. But I was not living in those golden years.

I remembered doing house calls in the late 1980s, after the startup of my veterinary hospital, to bring in some extra cash. The problem with going back to those days was obvious.

This time, I would not have access to my own pharmacy, lab testing equipment, diagnostic equipment, surgical instruments, etc. Reflecting back on my first job disaster—young, idealistic, new graduate, manipulated by a money-motivated scum bag—I also rejected the idea of becoming a white-coat corporate sellout. As I've explained, my early years as a solo practitioner were a costly learning curve, both financially and emotionally. My first business venture, with a zero-business plan, made the hospital ribbon cutting just a pat-on-the-back party with me picking up the tab. This time, I needed a much simpler plan. I wanted to make it bullet-proof.

And then I remembered something else. Most of those house calls were requests for home euthanasia. So I Googled.

Chapter Nineteen

The Bet

Don't be afraid of change, it's leading you to a new beginning.
—Anonymous

In my seven-year veterinary absence (other than CE to keep my California license valid), I found that requests for home euthanasia had skyrocketed. So much so in fact, a new branch had sprouted on the veterinary tree: pet hospice care that included new curriculum for best practice on euthanasia in the home environment.

I let that sink in for a minute. More surfing-the-web discoveries turned up third party websites recruiting veterinarians. These websites were driving traffic to match clients with veterinarians by zip codes. I had been living under a rock. The next certified training course was being offered in Loveland, Colorado, and I had just enough time to make all the arrangements. Three weeks later, after my connecting flight through Phoenix and a one-hour shuttle ride from the Denver airport, I was in Loveland. My jumpstart training would start first thing in the morning after breakfast. I could feel the butterflies flutter.

The trip to Colorado was a fruitful mini-vacation. It was nice to meet and talk with a small group of like-minded veterinarians, eat prepared meals together, and hang out in a quiet creature-comfort suite with no distractions. I soaked up the experience like a dehydrated bag of potato chips. As everyone parted ways, two days later, we would have new roads to navigate. Mothers would have control over their working lives by setting their own schedules, overworked vets found a magic pause button to rest and recover from fourteen-hour work days, and for a few weirdos like me, it was pseudo-retirement. We had a chance to dust off and morph into part-time freelance doctors. I already had the wheels—my trusty Outback Subaru. All I needed was the black bag. (Thank you, Amazon.) And just like that, I was mentally back in focus. Screw retirement.

I was starting from scratch. Time consuming phone calls to locate the best medical suppliers were followed by hours of busywork to open new accounts. The process of filling out forms and applications kept me waiting for months to collect all medical supplies and required permits and licenses. When I finally 'came out' to friends on Facebook that I was starting a house call practice, I didn't know what to expect. Old friends and previous clients cheered me on, glad that I was back in the saddle. To my new friends, collected over the last five years or so, I was still the owner of what people called "the doggy hotel." I couldn't really blame them. After all, I had formed the LLC with an identity of it being a place for dogs—The Dog Spa.

Before I could dash off and reclaim my professional dog tags, I needed to be free of my hotel duties. Backing up a bit, my declaration of freedom started in November 2016, when I promised myself that I would sell the hotel and close escrow by end of May or June at the latest, no matter what. This was my six months' notice of resignation. June was my deadline. I was getting out. I was beyond done; I wore the smell of burnt toast.

Ending up as another unlucky owner of a "too hot" vacation spot in Death Valley (my term for any desert landscape during the blazing summer months, starting in June) was not going to be the end of my story.

June is the kick-off month for a long hot summer of hell. Getting "heads in beds" (a popular coined term kicked into play by hoteliers with too many vacancies) is the holy grail of the hotel business. For restaurateurs and shopkeepers, the summer is no picnic for them either. The thought of sweating out another miserable summer in triple-digit temps and watching my bank account teeter into the red zone kept me up at nights. Wine, my knock-out drug of choice, was not working. During my sleepless nights, I fantasized a summer vacation at the beach—any beach.

By August, I had to admit defeat. After nine long, agonizing months of waiting for a sale I was a seller without a buyer. I complained to anyone with ears who would listen. By invitation, I spotted John at someone's party. He listened, but instead of pity, he had an idea. John was thinking outside of the box.

A jolly guy with an infectious smile, John enjoyed a playful presence. His longstanding career in public relations and marketing added flare to his credibility as a businessman. But John wasn't looking to buy any property when he asked to come for a visit. It was a triple digit July, so I told him to wear his swim trunks and come on over. I handed him a towel and we jumped into the cool pool, only 88 degrees. (It registered 110 degrees outdoors).

As we soaked and talked, John started sketching me the big picture. The hotel was less than two miles from a large cannabis grow site, and the city had sprouted thirteen pot dispensaries in less than two years Recreational use had made it onto California's ballot and passed. It was time to wake up and smell the cannabis opportunity. The new flower of promise in Desert Hot Springs also carried the badge of honor for being the first city in the state to grow the green weed.

Two hours later, our waterlogged bodies made it out of the pool. I told John I would think about it. It was not a rhetorical "think about it" blow off. I did think a lot about his idea. John wanted an opportunity that would twist me like a pretzel, 180 degrees. His offer was a bet-the-farm gamble. First, I had to bet on the City of Desert Hot Springs. Then, follow that with a second bet on John's abilities. A game of double jeopardy.

Chapter Twenty

Reboot

The pessimist complains about the wind; the optimist expects it to change; the realist adjusts the sails.
—William Arthur Ward

In my little town of Desert Hot Springs—population under 28, 000—the city only had one thing going for it, besides its stunning foothill views. Settlers in the 1800s discovered priceless hot water below the ground. The town sprung to life over one of earth's finest natural hot mineral aquifers. Wells tap down a few hundred feet to pump and fill alluring watering holes with the earth's naturally heated water. Underground water so hot, pools and hot tubs can be maintained at ideal temperatures year-round, saving natural gas for water heaters and appliances. The gas company goes without.

It was all a roar in the forties, fifties and sixties. Historians would point out its decline started in the seventies. Some blamed criminal activity. By 2007, fallen house prices made Desert Hot Springs a landlord's dreamland. For residents, it was becoming a neighborhood nightmare. Even before hitting rock bottom, the city had lost its charm as a tourist town. As the hotel business dried up, more and more buildings were boarded up and abandoned. It had become a picture-perfect town of neglect.

What started out as an affordable warm and sunny place for retirees and water-loving weekend guests—just a two-hour drive from LA—had slowly morphed into rundown and abandoned properties, a haven for drug dealers, and low-income housing. Years of poor city leadership that lacked any realistic plans for development had taken their ugly toll. Flip-flop city employees added to the grab bag of problems plaguing the city decades before I rode into town. No wonder I could afford to buy the old beat up hotel after it sat vacant for three years. Maybe it wasn't such a deal after all.

By 2011 the city was broke. At a much-anticipated city council meeting, residents lined the walls once all seats were taken. Our city manager would be ready to announce the city's bank balance. I don't remember the exact number, but bottom-of-the-barrel shockwaves filled the room. Even I had more than a measly four hundred and something bucks in my checking account. Over the next two years, the city cut services, salaries and staff in a desperate attempt to slash their annual budget from $19 million to $13.5 million. Someone in public works turned off the water supply to a park, turning the grass brown. And the city council voted to fill up a public swimming pool with dirt to strike the maintenance fees from the newly revised operating budget. The city was dead broke after decades of decline. I had to really wonder what I was doing here. I was not optimistic.

By 2014, after three long, dry years, the city had restored its fiscal obligations. Our operational budget was balanced, and city advisors seemed determined to start allocating monies into a reserve account. That same year, cannabis cultivation was put on the ballot for residents to decide. It was a bold, albeit desperate move to increase city revenues. An ordinance allowing cannabis cultivation in the light industrial zones sent an avalanche of "Yes" voters to the voting booth. Fence-sitters jumped off when first year projected revenues were greater than the city's revised annual budget. Cannabis cultivation ushered in new development, with its corresponding fees and sales tax revenue. A lot of people believed it could be a real game changer for the city. I was becoming one of them.

By 2016, two years after cannabis cultivation won approval, the city was swarming in blueprints and building permits. Onlookers watched as new construction sites started breaking ground. Even the largest controversial indoor grow facility—an eye-popping one million square feet—sailed through the approval process. There were up to seventy-nine projects in the pipeline at any given time. The planning department hired additional engineers and support staff, to handle the demand. Desert Hot Springs was humming with activity.

Our budding cannabis industry promised that its future workforce would look with favor on our resident population. So, the suits didn't blink an eye when the city asked that a minimum 25 percent of applicants be Desert Hot Springs new hires for trade jobs that paid well. Cannabis newcomers blew the cork off the bottle, giving us reason to believe that the medicinal properties of a strange-smelling plant that healed the sick might also heal the city. The backward town I landed in was now turning heads with hope and dollars signs. Desert Hot Springs, the Coachella Valley underdog, was starting to bark—loudly.

In 2018, a small dog park materialized. That was the neon sign that the city had not only stopped hacking community services; it was spending its precious new revenue to help build back our community. All the proof I needed to believe. I smiled with surprise as I drove by, never expecting to witness the ribbon-cutting of a new park in my poor little town. I still remembered the brown grass and empty swimming pool. It had been brutal to watch. Some townspeople had lost all hope. I was one of the hopeless.

Several weeks later, John and I reached an agreement. The dog-friendly Desert Hot Springs Inn put out a new "Welcome Guests" sign. We had a plan to attract 420 friendly travelers. Our redesigned website opened the doors for pet lovers and cannabis aficionados to unleash themselves from restrictive policies. We wanted our guests to relax in the creature comforts of home where dogs could jump on beds and couches and people could light up around the pool or patio at their leisure.

John had successfully sold his idea, but I was still on the hook to remain the hotel owner. I signed the operational agreement with high hopes—being the dreamer I am. Hope that my bet would turn me from a poor innkeeper to a wise investor. Relieved of my hotel duties, I had the wings to fly off to Loveland, Colorado. I had John to thank for my swift departure.

Chapter Twenty-One
Save A Pet

An activist is someone who cannot help but fight for something. That person is not usually motivated by a need for power or money or fame, but in fact is driven slightly mad by some injustice, some cruelty, some unfairness, so much so that he or she is compelled by some internal moral engine to act to make it better.
—Eve Ensler

I got my first taste of activism after the news broke the story in Denver, CO. I spent four years on the battleground fighting breed discrimination. It was a classic case of fear and ignorance. This was different. In the battle to save our town's beloved non-profit rescue organization, Save A Pet (SAP), from a hostile takeover, I came face to face with evil. Malinda Bustos was running a non-profit she named Humane Society of the Desert (HSOD). Looking back, plagiarizing the name Humane Society was an early clue of her motive to deceive the public. When this real-life scam artist got wind of an opportunity to seize the assets of Save A Pet in the summer of 2015, rumors that SAP was in jeopardy got real. By the time I received an urgent call for help, it was already too late.

For years, Bustos bankrolled her princess-like lifestyle—million-dollar house, Mercedes Benz and show horses—on dollars donated and estates bequeathed to her non-profit. She knew how to rub elbows with wealthy donors and put on glitzy fundraisers. Now she wanted to get her grubby hands on the impressive fortunes of SAP—just a few miles down the road. Time was up when Save A Pet was forced to move and find a new location for their dog kennels. That's when the black widow moved swiftly to spin a story and cast her web.

The Save A Pet saga began in 1981 when Mary Sydnes organized a small group she named "Friends of Needy Animals." Mary was determined to find a safe place to care for the unwanted strays that littered the streets. She put her mind and resources into fundraising and started the town's first thrift shop to generate some quick cash. Two years later, Mary purchased 1.6 acres with a house and a carport on 18th Avenue in Desert Hot Springs. By 1984, Save A Pet was incorporated and permitted by Riverside County to shelter fifty-five dogs. It was a non-profit animal rescue that limped along and struggled for many years, built mainly on the backs of volunteers and meager donations. There were management and compliance issues that plagued the rescue from its humble beginnings right up to its demise. It was the sheer will of the volunteers that kept the lights on, kennels cleaned, and strays from going hungry. Being the only game in town made Save A Pet the only safety net to prevent homeless pets from taking a one-way trip to the Riverside County Shelter death camp. It was backbreaking and lifesaving work. I was grateful for its mighty efforts.

Before the passing of the beloved founder, Mary Sydnes, in 2010, Save A Pet had earned such a good reputation in the community that it was not uncommon for long-time donors to bequeath estates and other valuable resources. After Mary's passing at age ninety-three, her resourceful Board of Directors voted to invest a substantial amount of working capital into their dream of building a state-of-the-art animal hospital. It was bold and ambitious and something our town desperately needed—a prize that Bustos desperately wanted.

After delays, setbacks and other unpleasant surprises, construction of the Animal Hospital of Desert Hot Springs was completed in the Spring of 2013. Ambitious undertakings had always been the spirit of Save A Pet. It was a proud moment Mary would miss, but one in which the whole town celebrated. We had Mary and her "Friends of Needy Animals" to thank for all of it. It was living proof of what a small group of like-minded people could accomplish. It was astonishing to witness how far the non-profit had succeeded—and devastating to watch it fail.

To this day the rest of the story remains somewhat of a mystery. The question everyone wanted an answer to was *why*. Why had SAP failed to secure a new location for the rescue when they had the resources to do so? The County had warned the organization one year earlier, due to a zoning issue, that they needed to relocate their kennel. However, the small house, converted to a cattery, could remain on the 1.6 acres. The clock was ticking for the Save A Pet dogs.

A perfect storm started brewing when Save A Pet board members accepted an invitation by Bustos. Recent resignations, set off by a newcomer on the board, had downsized SAP's board members from seven to only three. First, the three SAP members toured the well-manicured grounds surrounding the kennels and office space on the spacious five-acre HSOD property. Of course, they saw plenty of room for expansion and the very real possibly to relocate the SAP dogs. Heads were nodding up and down. Bustos had lured them onto the property with hints of a merger between the two non-profits. Then she just kept turning on the charm.

Next came an arranged-by-design meeting by MB, billed as a friendly meet-and-greet for the two boards to talk. That's when things got weird and fuzzy. The vice president of SAP, Chuck Bennett, described his "Yes" vote on the merger as only his willingness to move forward with special council to see if an agreement by both sides could be reached. Ann Woods, the treasurer, simply agreed with Chuck. Dirk Voss, the president, was absent (more about him later). So only two board members were in attendance—Chuck and Ann. The proposed meet and greet was a con job. Bustos had orchestrated the hostile takeover of SAP by recording fraudulent board minutes: two "Yes" SAP votes in favor of the merger and a unanimous "Yes" vote in favor by HSOD board members. None of it was remotely legal and it all could have been contested. But before opposition forces could mount an attack and hire legal counsel to prove that fraud had been committed, Ann had already lost her mind.

Ann was a gentle soul and now in her mid-seventies, a veteran volunteer of Save A Pet for decades. She was kept especially busy during kitten season when unwanted litters were dumped on her doorstep. As a seasoned grandma, she had mastered around-the-clock bottle feedings and general care of the newborns. Abandoned kittens, feral cats, and cats in need of medical care were Ann's thing—making her top management in the feline department. This cozy cattery of felines was Ann's soft spot, giving MB all the clout she needed. She demanded that Ann, the treasurer, hand over all the SAP bank accounts, passwords and keys to the safe—or else. Taking the fifty-seven SAP cats as her hostages, Bustos played and won a game of emotional blackmail.

As things went from bad to worse, no one in the small army of opposition, including myself, could stop Ann from caving into Bustos' hostile demands. As Ann's worst fears turned into panic, she lost all ability to see logic. Before we could retain legal counsel, SAP was in the hands of the devil. In exchange for handing over the keys to the SAP kingdom, Ann was granted permission to remain on the property and care for the cats. The scam of a merger left Ann and the cats out in the cold rain. Stripped of non-profit status and funding, Ann would be unable to manage the cattery. When this terrible news got out to the rescue community, the non-profit Kittyland stepped up to cover the last remains of SAP with an umbrella. The old Save A Pet sign on the property Mary had purchased came down. The cattery remains, adjacent to the vacant dog kennels. The new sign reads "Kittyland Cat and Kitten Rescue." RIP Save A Pet.

Bustos walked away with millions in SAP assets—including the recently built animal hospital—without a scratch. Voss resigned as President and was awarded an employment opportunity as the new hospital manager. (It didn't seem to matter that he had no previous job experience.) Naturally, Chuck and Ann would live on to rue that day they innocently said "Yes." Both honest to the core and devoted to the SAP mission, they shared many sleepless nights. Without suspicion, their trust made them easy targets for the con when SAP had become most vulnerable, weakened by the loss of key board members and under the gun by the county's threat to take action. Rebel forces could not stop the fatal blow to Save A Pet. Its fate ultimately rested in the hands of grandma Ann. She would not sacrifice the lives of those 57 needy felines. Who could really blame her?

On a lazy unsuspecting morning in the spring of 2018, Facebook messenger popped up with a message. Next, an email landed in my inbox—both from rebel forces. Something was up.

This news was received with doubtful eyes and a load of skepticism. All our previous attempts had failed to launch a complete investigation by the District Attorney. We had evidence of fraud and embezzlement three years ago. Although we did get the attention of Michael Hestrin, Riverside County DA, we were dumbfounded and furious when his office dropped the investigation less than two months later after interviewing several key witnesses. All inquiries as to why went unanswered by the DA's office. Mysteriously, Bustos managed to slip away from her accusers and continue with her business as usual. Like taking candy from a baby, she continued to defraud the public and steal their money. Worse than that, the Save A Pet dogs went missing once they were in her custody. She never wanted them or Ann's cats. Oh, how we hated her.

Chapter Twenty-Two

Breaking News

Little thieves are hanged but great ones escape.
—14th Century French Proverb

The breaking news was viewed with suspicion from the moment we heard it. In fact, it was too good to be true. Even if it was true, we all agreed Bustos would find a way to slither out of the accusations, like the snake we knew her to be. Like the last time we had her cornered. Or so we thought.

A decision was made to keep our ears to the ground and take no immediate action. We had to be sure before we joined forces with the new axe-to-grind rebels. Week after week, the story unfolded in the news. Video coverage emerged with damning testimonies by people on the HSOD payroll—proof that Bustos had ruled her kingdom with threats, intimidation and lies. If you worked for her, she owned you. Employees who wanted to keep their jobs learned not to disobey an order. Her slime-ball attorney mailed out cease and desist letters like candy on Halloween to anyone who threatened to expose her dirty little secrets. Until one day—the day she gave marching orders to a veterinarian. A feisty Midwestern cowgirl raised in a Mormon family. Someone who knew right from wrong. Someone who could not be bullied.

Dr. RR had been working at the animal hospital for about a year—long enough to watch Bustos bully hospital staff, take unnecessary risks to cut corners, and stuff her own pockets. That day, Bustos' commanding order violated the good doctor's ethics. When she refused to obey, the Botox queen launched an all-out threatening attack.

After a brief moment of shock, Dr. RR shot back with, "I quit! I don't have to work for you!" She pulled her medical license off the wall, packed her office and called her staff together—a staff that, over the course of a year, felt more like a family. They begged Dr. RR for a special meeting, pleading with her not to quit. They had a plan B.

It was a last-ditch effort, but they had nothing more to lose. If the plan failed, they all vowed to quit. The hospital staff decided to go around Bustos, writing letters to all the other HSOD board members. The letters put these HSOD members on notice. Listing a summary of grievances against Bustos, they delivered a grave ultimatum: She goes, or we all go.

The board responded, "Please give us three days. Don't quit."

This is not a tactic that would have worked for me and my comrades three years ago. We didn't have any leverage, like shutting down a two-million-dollar animal hospital. Besides, we absolutely had no respect for her cherry-picked board members. At that board table, decency and the truth were two empty seats. After all, they had voted for the hostile takeover, never responded to Bustos' many critics, and accepted her abhorrent behavior. Even her husband was a voting member—a den of deceit with board members chosen among their wealthy friends. Bustos as the president gave us every reason to believe the board was a rigged stage of corruption. A lost cause. Fortunately, the hospital staff had not been in the trenches fighting her over Save A Pet three years earlier. They did not suffer that hangover of defeat. Marching forward, the hospital staff put their faith on the board table. Their ultimatum worked.

Whether this latest crisis was the impetus for worried HSOD board members taking swift action to look like the good guys, or overt criminal investigation of the non-profit, outsiders may never really know. What becomes clear is that the board took action to avoid a catastrophic shutdown of the animal hospital. Three days later they had ousted Bustos and her puppy dog husband. The board pledged an alliance to the hospital staff and offered their full support.

As if this was not shocking enough, I waited a few weeks before I could believe it. I wanted more details and the media delivered in spades. Earthquake-sized shockwaves hit when the HSOD board claimed to have turned over financial records and other evidence to the sheriff—proof of Bustos' embezzlement and fraud. They also courted the media to publicly air her dirty laundry. This emboldened board seemed ready to acknowledge the testimonies of Bustos' accusers and do the right thing.

Malinda Bustos first crossed my path just a few weeks before that fateful day when she loaded the SAP dogs into her van. What happened next, and the toils that prompted other chapters to be written, remains my motivation to put ink on paper. It's my wholehearted attempt to channel outrage, in a productive way, in hopes that others will find their own voice of courage in their fight for justice.

Soon after Ann surrendered, a lovely older lady returned to the SAP property only to find Ann and the cats. She had come to adopt one of the SAP dogs named Frodo. Although

Ann took Bustos's threats to harm the cats seriously if she didn't get everything she wanted, she still believed the dogs went to the HSOD shelter. With Ann's direction, the woman drove off to claim the dog she had been visiting, Frodo. The shelter attendant on duty that day simply said Frodo had gone to his forever home. Although disappointed and a little heartbroken, she was pleased someone had adopted him. She learned the ruthless truth on Facebook. It was all a lie.

Soon after Bustos had taken control of the hospital, horrible news was being leaked. Frodo was put down. An order by Bustos was the only reason given. Frodo's forever home was in heaven. In her conquest, the dogs were just disposable baggage. Only Ann's cats had remained safe. The cattery was allowed to occupy the rickety old property Mary Snydes purchased decades ago. The blond ponytail con artist had no use for it. There was nothing left of Mary's rescue. Nothing except for revenge.

Chapter Twenty-Three

Opportunity Knocks

*Your biggest break can come from never quitting.
Being at the right place at the right time can only happen
when you keep moving toward the next opportunity.*
—Arthur Pine

I was just days away from finishing up my list of doctor chores and pages of paperwork—checking off all items needed to revoke my retirement status—when Dr. RR replied. The notification came on Facebook Messenger, the first place I went looking for her. I was thrilled when I did a Facebook search and a photo popped up matching her cowgirl reputation. I had also heard about her special interest in equine surgery. Yep, all there in her bio. Although reliable information had been leaking out about the takedown for weeks, I wanted more details. As soon as she responded, I knew we would talk. It's a vet thing; veterinarians share a special bond—like war veterans. We have fought some of the same battles and survived with the scars to prove it. Besides that, we shared the common gender bond. Dr. RR spilled the beans with exasperated relief. Our Facebook introduction quickly morphed into the trenches of collaboration. A common enemy will do that.

After Dr. RR's twenty-minute breathless rant, I jumped in to assure her that she had indeed been working in Crazy Land. Unforgiving behavior endured by the hospital staff reported as irrational, threatening and demeaning was validated my own previous dark encounters with Bustos. During our heated conversation, we both expressed fears that the reformed HSOD board might cave in to Bustos' threats—especially after we learned the exiled president had retaliated by hiring a blue-suit lawyer.

Bustos claimed that the board's vote, which removed her from the throne, violated proper procedure. Beyond all imagination, this visit by karma was the most delicious payback possible. A chapter right out of Cruella de Vil's own playbook. Only this time, despite more lies and manipulation, the HSOD stewards moved swiftly to defend their decision and hired their own blue suit. Making it clear they were not backing down. Not this time.

I just about *begged* Dr. RR to stay the course and give this courageous board a chance to perform on its promises. Not only had they removed Bustos, they voluntarily agreed to share the sordid details with the media to publicly shame her. By all appearances, they seemed determined to make things right. It was time to buckle up, so I made the courageous doctor a promise: Anytime you need anything call me. And she did.

Everything on my Thursday "to do" list got canned when the good doc called in a panic around 7:30 in the morning. I was still sipping coffee when my cell phone started buzzing. Without a second thought, I said yes. It was the promise I had made her two weeks earlier. Now she was in a pinch and on her way to urgent care after suffering abdominal pain and flu-like systems for the last two days. The animal hospital would be unlocking its doors at 8:00 a.m. as patients started to arrive. I said I could get there within the hour. I hung up the phone in a state of shock-like disbelief.

In forty-five minutes, I would be in the parking lot of a veterinary hospital once under occupation by a tyrant. It was surreal. Of course, it was not the backdoor of my twenty-five-year-old veterinary hospital. That doorway was joyfully occupied by familiar staff and patients waiting to see me. I had no clue what would be waiting for me behind this door. I just knew I had to go. I could not let that brazen veterinarian down; she was my hero.

Although Dr. RR had a well-trained support staff, I was challenged by my veterinary departure and unfamiliar surroundings. I could not recall once familiar drug dosages and knew nothing about newer pharmaceuticals being prescribed. I constantly asked for the whereabouts of this or that and if they had such and such. I was a befuddled doctor moving in slow motion. Under the circumstances, the staff appeared to appreciate that I had shown up on an hour's notice. Clients and needy patients would not go without veterinary care. Clearly, I was better than nothing.

After making it through the morning, I was more worried about the ailing doctor's health than anything else. I did not want to play another day in the land of lost veterinarians. Fortunately, I didn't need to. That vet is one tough cowgirl. She was back in the saddle the following afternoon, commanding her staff. They adored her. I was really starting to like her, too. Two weeks later we met for lunch. We had a lot to talk about.

During our rapid-fire conversation, we talked and chewed at the same time. We shared bits and pieces about ourselves and the glory of an enemy's defeat. Save A Pet's animal hospital was finally out of the clutches of a ruthless dictator and had fallen into the loving, compassionate hands of an ethical veterinarian. I was overjoyed to have gotten my foot in the door and wanted to keep it there. The thought that I would be counted among the courageous souls that outlasted a tyrant, to reclaim the hospital and restore its reputation, put me over the moon. I was the new gun for hire; Dr. RR only had to ask. By the end of our lunch meeting, she did.

I knew that if I was offered a position, my work requirements could be real deal breakers. First, I needed a work environment that kept me out of the surgery suite. It's not a place I feel cool, calm and collected. Secondly, I needed the freedom to use my own medical judgment with respect to vaccine protocols, pet food diets and natural supplements. I wanted to step back into the shoes that filled the void in most pet hospitals—the holistic vet. Both were non-negotiable.

Dr. RR was not alarmed about my lack of surgical skills and ardent desire to keep it that way. She was naturally drawn to surgery and loved it. Next, she said that while she didn't focus on the "holistic stuff," she'd be okay with letting me claim that space. I dodged both bullets that afternoon and there was more good news. The hospital was not owned by corporate conglomerates, like Veterinary Centers of America (VCA) or Banfield, so I would not be strangled by a corporate leash. Even better, The Animal Hospital of Desert Hot Springs enjoyed non-profit status, making it a rare bird in the veterinary world. Its profits would trickle down to support animal rescue efforts. By joining the ranks of this hospital staff, I'd finally be generating some revenue for myself and, at the same time, pouring profits into the rescue organization. That was a crowd-crazy home run for me, both personal and professional. The stolen legacy of Save A Pet was finding its redemption. And it all started when an adamant doctor took her power back and said "No!" "No, I won't do that!" The *No* that changed everything.

I was grateful to start my first day with three clients on the books waiting to see me. It was the confidence booster I really needed. Fortunately, I had formed alliances within the rescue community after my relocation to the Coachella Valley six years earlier. When I announced on Facebook that I had accepted a part-time veterinary position, within two days I had over one hundred likes, loves, and wows. Friends shared it with friends—the word was out. It was all the PR I would need.

I felt gratifying pride to see familiar faces in the lobby and exam rooms. I soon realized that I never lost my passion for veterinary medicine. I simply lost myself. After a soft knock on the door, before entering, my voice went on autopilot. It uttered four simple words: "Hi, I'm Doctor Terifaj." Words of introduction not spoken since I left my roots in Orange County. I knew it would only confuse people.

Maybe I was confused, too.

Chapter Twenty-Four

Ace in the Hole

The people who are crazy enough to think they can
change the world are the ones who do.
—Walter Isaacson

During the budget crisis of 2011, Riverside County Animal Control reared its ugly head. Another battle was brewing. Penalizing amendments were woven into existing animal control ordinances that had financial roots digging into the pockets of dog owners. Obvious to many, the county was having its own cash shortage, and planned to balance their budget on the backs of dog owners not in compliance with new regulations. Of course, that was not *their* story. They cited the failure of existing ordinances (standard for most cities) to lessen the burden of shelter expenses. Failure to reduce impounds (strays and unwanted litters) was maxing out kennel space and increasing costs. Continued failure of their recordkeeping system (which was on them) to generate revenue from license fees was also a problem. Pet owners found not to be in compliance with the updated ordinance would face fines of up to four hundred bucks—*per pet*. Fines that could exceed a thousand bucks for multiple pet households. Sure, this would fix everything—especially in poor neighborhoods, which they targeted. People struggling to pay the rent, also struggled to feed the family dog. A goldmine of non-compliance issues.

The poorer cities like Desert Hot Springs and Indio were the first targets on Riverside County's hit list. Meter maids (as we called them) walked down the streets and up individual driveways, blowing their whistles. They were even seen peering over fences. They had only to see a dog or hear it barking to leave citations on the front door. Because of their inept recordkeeping, even dog owners with paid and up-to-date licenses were being cited. Cited residents and activists like me were in an uproar. Phone complaints rolled into the city daily. And when one of the city council members who did not own a dog was also cited (a voice-recorded barking dog device was activated by a motion detector), that was the last straw. The chaos entered the realm of the absurd.

I got a meeting with city officials to explain that California law only required that dogs be current on their rabies vaccines—nothing more. Generating one hundred-dollar fines for each failure to microchip, spay/neuter, vaccinate for rabies, and pay pet licenses fees was not mandated by the state. This imposed policy was the brainchild of Riverside County. Their law enforcement tactics did nothing more than cause pet owner panic. Some people started hiding their dogs. Others let them go to avoid potential fines. One guy, after receiving a twelve hundred dollar fine, reportedly shot all three of his dogs in a failed attempt to avoid paying the fines. What we truly needed were Spanish-speaking social workers to help educate the Latino population, community low cost spay/neuter services, and help with transportation for the elderly and disabled to get the services they needed. After several weeks of being a loud vocal critic at city council meetings, I got a call from the mayor. I immediately said *Yes!*

Riverside County Animal Control held meetings every two months to deliver staff reports and other news to the cities they serviced. Each city sent a representative to occupy one of the eight seats at the conference table—each city except Desert Hot Springs. Since 1962, the year the city was incorporated, that seat had remained empty. Apparently, none of the city council members wanted to draw straws for that seat at the table. I suppose they found other committees more interesting or important. So, at the mayor's invitation, I went. I had a lot to talk about and nothing they wanted to hear.

Keeping my ear to the ground, I wasn't falling for their phony staff report. Riverside County Animal Shelter, after all, operated as a kill shelter. They were not committed to the no-kill movement, unlike the cherished Palm Springs Animal Shelter. So their pie chart was divided like this:
- number of impounds
- number of animals euthanized due to injuries
- number of animals euthanized due to illness
- number of "healthy" euthanasias

After attending several of these meetings and always finding the count of "healthy" euthanasias to be zero, I started to smell a rat. So, I invited one of my new desert rescue friends to lunch. Lisa had chosen a restaurant with a beautiful outdoor patio and we picked the table offering the perfect amount of sunlight next to calming sounds of a waterfall. By the time our delicious salads were served, the conversation was doing nothing for my appetite. I was smelling a whole department of lying rats.

Lisa explained that several months earlier, she was given access to what people called the "back room" at the Riverside shelter—a room of cages filled with a collection of dogs and cats waiting to have their lives ended that very same day. It was the infamous "kill room" and their number was up. Lisa was on a hunt for a small dog. She was directed to three small dogs in one of the kill cages. They were scared and huddling together. Overwhelmed by sadness she grabbed all three. They did not die before 5 p.m. that day. I knew Lisa would be at the next meeting to speak during public comments. What I didn't know was her plan to bring one of the three pups. Her voice trembled as she waved the black Chihuahua mix up into the air for all to see. Verified by her own vet, it was not sick or injured. Not a single city representative, nor her accusers, replied. There was silence until it was my turn to speak.

I singled out the pathetic staff veterinarian, demanding to know exactly what his definition of a "healthy" euthanasia was. Knowing that I was a veterinarian, here is the translation of his doctor-talk explanation. Healthy impounds deemed not to be "sick" on arrival can spike fevers with snotty nasal discharge or coughs days later. What he was referring to are the contagious, upper viral respiratory infections cats can be exposed to in kennel or cattery environments, and the notorious kennel cough dogs can be exposed to in indoor kennels while being boarded. He just admitted that his shelter—a giant indoor kennel—was teeming with infectious bugs. To catch one was a death sentence. What about GI symptoms like diarrhea or vomiting? What if the animal was so stressed it growled or threatened to bite?

Lisa's frightened young black Chihuahua mix had this warning written on her shelter cage card: growls, may bite. *What if* was the elephant in the room. I quickly shot back: "So, you are saying that once they get sick, because they are exposed to disease in your shelter, they are added to the 'animals euthanized due to illness' category. Right?"

If someone had had a camera pointed at me, this would have been the photo caption:

Outraged veterinarian takes down Riverside County's staff veterinarian for his pathetic rationale to justify the shelter's reported euthanasia statistics, claiming they do not kill healthy dogs and cats.

I pointed to the evidence in the room—the black Chihuahua mix Lisa was cradling in her arms. "Does that dog look like a zero?"

That showdown cost me a seat at the table. Technically, the Riverside rule makers had the power to boot me off and kick me over to the public comment sector—which they did, after they informed the mayor (who had appointed me) that only sitting council members could serve as representation. Instead of a noisemaker like me, their complaint got them Joe McKee. And Joe was on my side. He was a mover and a shaker, and we shared some history. Joe was my ace in the hole.

I first met Joe when he was in campaign mode to win a seat on the city council a few years back. I was so impressed with his sincerity and knowledge about the many problems facing the city, I was happy to join the ranks of his supporters—and write a check, too. After he was elected, I teamed up with Joe to volunteer my time to help with one of his projects—piles of trash and dumped items that had been collecting on vacant lots for decades. The city had never successfully tackled this problem and, being a new hotel owner, it was plain bad for my new business, too. No one wants to visit a ghetto, and Joe was sympathetic about the city's struggles to attract tourists.

So we started the Pick-Up Crew. One of the larger hotels with a kitchen agreed to feed the crew a hearty breakfast every Saturday morning before we went trash picking. During breakfast, Joe gave us city updates and discussed the issues the council was reviewing and voting on that month. I became the mouthpiece for all matters that concerned pet owners. While most people just wanted to complain about our downtrodden town, we were the hopeful souls that wanted to believe in its potential and be part of its revitalization. It felt better not to complain. It felt better to believe. And we believed in Joe.

Joe was already fired up about the pet fines and dealing with that issue. Keeping the pressure on, the city attorney poured over the contract the city had with Riverside, discovering two major errors. First, there had been no public service announcement to inform our residents. So they were in violation from the start of enforcement. Even worse, they had failed to inform city management and get the signatures they needed for approval. Was it really just a careless oversight or another blatant disregard for truth and facts?

After I brought Joe up to speed on some other shelter issues I was grappling with, we started attending the meetings together. The county's antics had awakened the city to a sleeping giant. Joe had already proven himself to be the most dedicated, hard-working city council member on the planet, and I was only too happy to volunteer my expert testimony. Joe had the muscle of fortitude, and I brought the expertise. The idiotic county was in for some trouble.

Before I was demoted, I took note when a city council member from Rancho Mirage popped up to question the shelter's criteria for the determination of dog aggression. Rumor had it they were destroying dogs they deemed dangerous—a decision made by a staff member. This city representative wanted more details concerning their qualifications to make an accurate behavioral assessment. Since they did not employ skilled dog trainers or an animal behaviorist, the answer was the same—a staff member. That narrowed it down to their worthless veterinarian, a kennel attendant or an office worker.

Here was another splatter of blood on their hands. The growl or bark of a fearful dog was deemed aggressive. Clearly, Lisa had the proof. Just like the coughing dog or the sneezing cat—both deemed to be ill. They were looking for any way to justify the kill, thus keeping "healthy euthanasias" to a big fat zero on the pie chart. It was nothing more than public appeasement. They would not be depicted as the bad guys. The polite smiles and silence of the other council members proved they were just bodies showing up for another boring meeting. I didn't expect anything to change.

After that meeting, I singled out the councilman from Rancho Mirage and tapped him on the shoulder. I politely asked if he had a few moments to talk with me. I just really wanted to thank him for speaking out and expressed my own angst on the subject and other troubling issues, like the pet fines. He seemed surprised about citations being doled out in other cities. Knowing that Rancho Mirage was a rather affluent area, it made sense to me that the county decided to spend its resources in the more disadvantaged areas. Besides, ruffling the feathers of people spending their days on the golf course could get ugly. But that's not *why* he didn't know. In a puff of smoke, the genie was out of the bottle. It really did seem too good to be true. He granted me a name and a phone number. And I called the City of Rancho Mirage the next day.

I spoke with the department head in charge of animal control. Daisy seemed pleased to take my call as I fired away with my list of questions. One by one, she handed me the keys to the castle. First, she gave me the budgeted expense for a single animal control officer (salary, insurance, and benefits) and associated vehicle costs. Then she shared the annual revenue received by providing license applications through the city—all residents were required to keep dog tags current. Lastly, we discussed their modified shelter contract with Riverside County. It was the policy of Rancho Mirage to attempt and identify all lost pets by contacting the owners and keeping them safe until the officer could drive them home. Not only was it the right thing to do, it helped cut down on impound fees (which, at the time of this writing, was a cost to the city of two hundred dollars per dog). Skirting the ride to the shelter also kept the pet owner from paying bail money. When you add those costs up, its double-dipping. The city pays impound fees when pet owners cannot be identified, and pet owners are saddled with the bail. It's a real win-win for the county and a bad experience for everyone else—including the family dog. The very prospect that other cities could follow the lead, a big step away from the County jail system, was my wish from the Rancho Mirage genie. It was a wish that would come true nearly four years later.

In the several years that passed after that magical Rancho Mirage phone call, three things happened. In fact, they had to happen before good fortune could strike. First, Joe had taken the copycat Rancho Mirage project under his wing. He saw the value right away. But in my heart of hearts, it was a pipe dream without adequate funding. And I believed Joe would eventually lose interest without the funds.

Next, budding revenues from the cannabis industry started to pay off. Finally, our dysfunctional city manager got the boot. A retired police captain replaced him, and his first-rate management skills were getting things done. Joe got him on board for the project to move forward.

Years of poor city management and ding dongs that kept winning votes on city council seats were all you needed to start a train wreck. Add to that the collateral damage of the 2008 – 2009 recession and I was on that train, too. Although I was still fighting the gloom and doom when I arrived in 2011, the clouds were finally lifting. It was 2015 and the sun was shining.

Chapter Twenty-Five

Joe's Plan

*The things you are passionate about are not random,
they are your calling.*
—Fabienne Fredrickson

Joe called and wanted to meet. I knew he was bringing me a copy of the proposal he and Walt Myer, a public safety commissioner, had been working on the past two years—overhauling the city's contract with the county shelter. By this time, it was much more than the scribbled two-page budget report Joe had started with. This time, he handed me a paper-filled three-ring binder. Unbeknownst to me, our new city manager, Chuck Maynard, had already given Joe's proposal the green light after he commissioned John Holcomb. John was a special projects manager, charged to research the full scope of Joe's proposal. Its budget and all the "how to" steps needed to be worked out. John would dig in for the next six months before completing his analysis. In that binder was a well-researched and detailed document. It was so much more than my Rancho Mirage wish coming true.

Page by page, the mandate advocated for the general care and welfare of the animals. It went far beyond Rancho Mirage's free-ride-home policy for all pets with ID. When put to the vote, our city council returned five unanimous "Yes" votes. That night the city of Desert Hot Springs broke tradition. Recognizing its need to break away from the county was a bold and daring move. That vote was permission to write rules and regulations that supported our values—our community. Reinvented animal control policies would be tucked under the enforcement wing of our competent police department. These would be the cool animal cops. Their badges picked up our strays and chased down bad pet owners. (Soon you will meet Flower.)

As written, Joe's plan plugged the holes of county absenteeism with two full-time animal control officers seven days a week. For dogs roaming the streets and those animals injured, calls to Animal Control after 2 p.m. and weekends would no longer go unanswered. The recorded Riverside County message saying to call back on Monday mornings after 9 a.m. was deleted, putting an end to countless hours of past neglect. Joe's plan included a budget for all calls, including weekends up to 5:30 p.m., to be answered. Other than Palm Springs Animal Control services, no other city in the Coachella Valley had ever attempted such a feat. What had once seemed impossible was made possible. To all the doubters, get rid of your excuses. And get to work!

After reviewing John's data, the city manager signed off on an estimated $180,000 to fund the rehabilitation of an abandoned building in the city's public works yard. The project detailed the rehab of a two-thousand-square-foot brick building to be used for Animal Control. This facility would provide office space, twelve indoor/outdoor dog kennels, a cattery and play yard with misters for the dogs in summer months. Lost and found pets would be safely housed for a minimum of four days, or longer as space allowed, for owners to be reunited with lost family pets. It was all I had hoped for and much more. Only one thing was missing: a reality check. What was the plan for sick or injured animals entering the newly remodeled Animal Care and Control Center on Hacienda Avenue?

In a sit-down meeting with the city manager, I asked that very question. A professed animal lover himself, Chuck (a retired police captain) assured me all medical needs would be addressed. However, there were no specifics, only the mention of working together with The Animal Hospital of Desert Hot Springs—still under siege by the sinister hands of Bustos. I was dumbfounded. Although Joe knew what I had told him three years earlier about Save A Pet was true, it was too late. It seemed that city staffers were already under Bustos' spell. So my offer to assist in the development and polices of the new animal control facility was just a bark at the moon. With a big gulp, I swallowed my pride. It was time to move on.

I took some comfort knowing that Desert Hot Springs had just hammered the first nail in the county shelter's coffin. I was proud of that and hopeful other cities would want to follow in our footsteps—adding more nails. In just two short months after spotting that first Animal Control truck on patrol, I got all the proof I needed to know the mandate was real. The proof was an abandoned dog soon to be named Flower. After one of our Animal Control officers picked her up, she got a ride straight to the Animal Hospital of Desert Hot Springs. I was on duty the morning she came in.

Chapter Twenty-Six

Date with Destiny

Adopt, if you can't adopt, foster, if you can't foster, volunteer, if you can't volunteer, donate, if you can't donate, educate.
—Anonymous

Negotiations between our new Animal Control Department and The Animal Hospital of Desert Hot Springs were already under way when the Animal Care and Control Center opened in the Spring of 2018. I was still keeping my distance with one eye open. I kept my bench seat warm on the sidelines until that fateful day when Dr. RR and her staff threatened to walk out. That memo had real teeth with the power to push board members between a rock and a hard place. First, the boulder-sized rock: A public explanation to answer the mysterious *why*. What happened that caused the complete shutdown of an animal hospital? Or the hard place: Wake up to the rotten, smelly elephant in the room. Both were newsworthy headlines. The Board chose which headline they wanted the public to read. Now, I was off the sidelines and ready to play.

By the time I started working for Dr. RR in July 2018, she was busy working on a budget to provide veterinary services for the department of Animal Control. Just as the city manager had promised. I still had no affiliation with the new Animal

Control and Care Center, nor had I visited the facility during its Grand Opening. I felt betrayed by city staff that heeded the warning by Bustos that I was "bad news." Sure, I was "bad news" for evildoers like her and others. I don't hesitate to point fingers at them. So, I just drove by the city yard and gazed at the rehabbed project under construction for months (a convenient three minutes from my house). I took satisfaction just watching its progress. When I finally entered that facility, it was a lot more than my curiosity knocking on the door. I was an un-retired, back to work, veterinarian caring for a patient in their custody. It was my job to be there.

Roughly two weeks after I started seeing appointments at the animal hospital, I walked through the treatment room looking for some damn thing, again, when I noticed an animal control officer standing there in full uniform. I stopped to look down and see what was standing at the end of a leash. I knew this day would come. I knew it would be difficult. Officers are tasked to pick up the injured, the neglected and the unwanted. A lot more than lost dogs getting a safe ride home. Clearly, the dog at the end of this leash was not a family's beloved pet. This was a dog no one cared about. No one would come looking for this dog.

The skinny, sad-looking pit bull had all the trimmings of a backyard breeding bitch with a sign around her neck: "Pit bull puppies only $50!" I was disgusted by the neglect and angered by the carelessness and human greed to pocket a few bucks—thwarting society's advancement toward the No Kill movement. (Once again, I'm reminded of the societal burdens irresponsible people heap upon the compassionate shoulders of the fixers.) I watched as this mama dog received our standard treatment for parasites and an antibiotic for her infected skin. True to his word, and my satisfaction, the city manager had factored in a budgeted amount for all impounds to be examined by a veterinarian. This budget would also pay out medical costs up to $110 per animal. Covering costs for a set amount of veterinary care was an unprecedented action by our city, or any city, as far as I knew. It was a remarkable moment to witness it happening. I never dreamed it possible. Especially not in Desert Hot Springs, the poor stepchild of Palm Springs. Tears tell the truth. I snuck outside to cry happy ones.

After her allocated dollars were spent, the dog was on her way to visit the new animal control building, just five minutes away. But she looked so bad I just knew she would require additional veterinary care if she had any hope of being adopted. I also worried about the limited number of days she would be allowed to stay at the animal control facility before her fate would be determined. The city staff had reached out and built an impressive network of non-profit rescue organizations to relocate dogs after a four-day hold was placed on them. They were doing an amazing job of relocating unclaimed strays—keeping them safely out of the Riverside shelter. There was no time to waste. I was a born fixer.

The city's revised contract with the county shelter kept the option open to transfer—at the city's discretion—any animal they needed to relinquish. Everyone understood the County was the last resort, but it was the best we could do. And it was a lot more than any other city in Riverside County was willing to tackle. The next day, I listened to my instincts. I went to see that miserable bag of bones.

It was a late afternoon on Friday when I knocked on the door of Animal Control. I delivered my medical judgment, expressing my concerns, to the animal care technician and animal control officer on duty. I asked to take the battered pit bull home for observation over the weekend and return her on

Monday. But there was no precedent for my request. When I got the "blah blah blah" response about how they did not have the authority to allow me to take the dog, I persisted. Twenty minutes of debate later, they agreed. It was the right thing to do for the dog. Screw formalities. In time, I was sure my oddly strange request would fill a new page in their procedure book. After all, we were making history in the Coachella Valley.

After the observational weekend I spent with the seemingly quiet and shy puppy producer, she left me unmistakable clues: voracious appetite, excessive water drinking and peeing a river. Yet, she was a boney fifteen pounds underweight. All the pieces fit this puzzle—confirmed with lab testing first thing Monday morning at the hospital. Next, I posted pictures of the newly diagnosed diabetic dog on Facebook with my pleas to find a foster home. I needed someone responsible and capable of giving insulin injections twice daily every twelve hours. That post also received lots of likes, wows and hearts. The comments were heartwarming, and the many shares appreciated, but no one wanted to step into those shoes. No one until a dog trainer I knew, and respected, left me a comment. She was interested. She was also seven months pregnant. I was pretty sure there would be second thoughts once she asked her hubby.

Chapter Twenty-Seven

Flower

Alone we can do so little; together we can do so much.
—Helen Keller

After being released from the confines of a noisy dog kennel, the homeward bound pit bull slept and rested in a quiet family home with her very own cozy dog bed—complete with five-star room service. The real dog that emerged was a rambunctious love bug with the curiosity of a daredevil cat—nose into everything, mostly to smell the butts of all newly encountered furry things. In full disclosure I also told Tabitha Davies of her aggressive interest to meet my feline, Kit Kat, hiding under my bed. Not yet knowing the true behavior of this dog, Kit Kat remained in lockdown the entire weekend. It was a chaotic two days for all concerned, except my new house guest. She had the run of the house and me. But my skillset was only the medical part of her rehabilitation. All hope was counting on Tabitha's expertise to drill in the commands—Sit, Stay, Down and Leave It—deep into her gray matter. No sane person would want to take on a "medical needs dog" with the unbridled energy of a two-year-old kid. Tabitha would have her hands full—especially with her own baby's due date only two months away.

After starting her on insulin at the hospital, Animal Control retrieved my weekend-long, vacationing canine and returned her to the shelter. I stopped by on my lunch hour to go over all the instructions with the staff on duty. They seemed willing and ready to administer the insulin at scheduled times and feed only the special diet I had prepared. It would be several days before Tabitha had the time and space to take on another project. On that day I got to the shelter early and, while waiting for Tabitha to arrive, learned that the canine—Jane Doe—had taken on an identity by the name of "Flower." I didn't question the "who" and "why" of that particular name. Obviously, the animal control staff had gone the extra mile for this special needs dog. Naming her was an act of dignity. It showed their compassion. To them she was more than the dog in Kennel Number 7. It made me smile.

After a brief introduction, Flower was leashed and led to a parked car waiting for her. Tabitha sat next to her in the back seat as the driver (daddy-to-be) adjusted the doggy seat belt. I stood in awe as I watched them wave and drive away. This was real teamwork or, as they say, it takes a village. Like children, dogs are the innocent victims of parental neglect and poverty. Finally, my professional career found the welcome mat to serve the have-nots. My medical degree was never about the money. It was a deep desire to make a difference. Find a problem you want to solve. This was mine.

Flower wasted no time for a proper meet-and-greet invitation. Tabitha was about to witness Flower's overzealous behavior on her own turf. The potbelly pig in the yard only garnered a shocking stare, like "what is that thing?" But once securely inside the front door, she launched her nose-tail dive into the smelly zone of all four resident dogs. She had shown that same behavior in the play yard while at the shelter. This rapid-fire smell job could be offensive to a first date, let's-take-our-time type of dog. These shy wallflower dogs will not be amused and, if stressed, there is the danger of a protective strike. But like what the shelter staff had observed, and videotaped, Tabitha soon confirmed. Flower's intent was more like, "I'm the life of the party; let's play!"

So, she passed the first test. However, her next discovery did not go well. One of Tabitha's cats, Jack, threatened war when Flower stuck her nose under his tail end where it clearly did not belong. When her other house cat, Einstein, witnessed this offensive act, he reared up on both hind legs and vocalized before launching his attack. Fortunately, both humans quickly intervened before any real damage was done. Initial behavioral assessment: Flower loves people, all dogs are her BFF's, she doesn't like the smelly pig in the yard, and cats are obviously evil.

The City of Desert Hot Springs set the bar high when they voted in a bold plan to re-invent the failed outsourcing of their animal control duties. This demonstrated the city's refusal to turn a blind eye to the problems outsourcing had created for our community. We knew, as a city, we had to do better. Moving ahead, city staffers calculated the risks involved if we failed to meet our objectives. Not surprisingly, there were unexpected setbacks and budget overruns—adding to everyone's anxiety. Within several months of tackling the remodel of an old outdated building, the estimated budget of $180,000 was not even in the ballpark. All in all, the city would go the extra mile to find the financing for an additional $160,000. Other delays in planning pushed the opening date months into the unknown future. Every new delay was a date with doubt. As the project kept moving forward, the doubts eventually faded away.

Once our animal control policies had become fully operational, Joe sat down to read reports and crunch the numbers. The data exceeded all expectations for our first six months. In previous years, the city on average recorded one thousand impounds at a cost of $150 per animal. Our animal control department slashed impounds at the County shelter by a whopping 80 percent—that's $120,000 added back into the city's budget. Review of the yearly contract for County services felt like a robbery—billed $300,000 for staff working less days and fewer hours. Much of that money would also stay in the city's coffers. Money that added more services and better staffing to make our animal control a top-notch operation.

But this was never just about cutting costs to the city budget. The ultimate goal was to provide animal control services of value to an underserved community with a mission to keep impounds safely out of the jaws of Riverside County. Our second chance measures did that and more. And if we could do it, no other city had an excuse not to try. Flower would be just one of many to find a second chance in this new village of hope.

Special thanks to Joe McKee. Your physical six feet, seven inches made you a giant by size in my five feet, one-inch eyes. But here's the better definition of a true giant using the Merriam-Webster dictionary: "Legendary humanlike being of great stature and strength." No one did more to advance a broken city in the five-year seat you occupied on Desert Hot Springs' city council.

Nothing about Joe would ever settle for the status quo. We had that much in common.

Chapter Twenty-Eight

First Call

*Don't take every challenge as a problem;
take every problem as a challenge.*
—Anonymous

The call came early in the morning as I was sipping my coffee. I quickly learned I was talking to the worried owner of an elderly cat. She complained that her cat had exhibited signs of illness off and on, but always seemed to "rally" and start eating again. That did not seem to concern the woman calling me. However, Tiger Lily had started to cry a lot in last few days. So, she knew it was time to do something. Not knowing exactly what creature was waiting for me, I knocked softly on the door that afternoon and nervously waited for it to open.

Tiger Lily was a long-haired Siamese—probably a beauty in her day. Now her thin hair-coat hung over her boney framework. All of about five pounds, she was a ruff measurement of skin and bones, frail and gaunt and indeed making distressing vocal sounds. I tempered my tone and dismissed the "Why didn't you ask for help months ago?" question. Palliative care to make her more comfortable was out of the question. The cat had not eaten in over a week and was dying a slow miserable death. *Euthanasia,* from Greek interpretation, confers a "good death." It is the practice of intentionally ending a life to relieve pain and suffering. In fact, veterinarians take such an oath to do just that—a privilege from which human doctors have been barred. This afternoon it would be my duty and privilege to end this poor cat's miserable life.

So the only words I allowed myself to speak signaled a warning to her owner: "In your cat's grave condition it may be difficult to locate a suitable vein to inject the drug—a barbiturate overdose." Indeed, I was headed for trouble.

I awakened from my veterinary coma feeling rusty and a little unsure of my capabilities. In need of some target practice, I wondered if my own dogs would volunteer. Well, they didn't exactly volunteer. Common injections, like vaccines, can be given subcutaneously (under the skin) or into the muscle. These injection sites make it an easy skill to acquire. But to "hit a vein" (common language for venipuncture) was a definite skill that required lots of practice and patience.

After shaving a patch of hair to expose a suitable vein, I felt transported back in time—just by using my new clippers. Next, I splashed rubbing alcohol on her inner thigh to get a better view. Later, when I described my panic to interested friends, I defined "tiny" vein as in the smallest toothpick you can imagine. It's a wonder I didn't faint.

Over the span of my veterinary career, and in my most recent home euthanasia training, I've learned that acting calm and confident in any situation is imperative. In other words, if the doctor loses it, so will the client or the patient. Things will go from bad to worse—guaranteed. The universe didn't care that day that it was my first call on the job. Brute forces would thrust me back into the closet of white coats and scrubs. It was going to be trial by fire and a wish for good luck.

The commonly used 22G needle blew the vein. Although I managed to hit the target, the tiny vein could not maintain its integrity and blood bubbled out into the surrounding tissue. Strike one. I stopped the bleeding and took a deep breath. I had to come up with another plan—and quickly. My recent training gave me the idea to try a smaller 25G needle—something that would not have been possible when I was in practice. We called it the "pink juice"—a viscous liquid colored by the distinguishing pink dye. The pink juice required the minimum size of 22G for proper flow. But in my new medical bag of tricks, I had the "blue juice." The new and improved euthanasia solution was more fluid and flowed with less force through the needle's diameter. I was about to get my first payoff from my training in Loveland, Colorado. Sure, the blue juice did cost more, but I trusted our instructor. If she thought the bottle was worth an extra twenty bucks compared to the old pink juice, I would not settle for less either.

With the smaller 25G and the wings of my guardian angel, the vein did not blow this time. Pushing firmly on the plunger I was able to administer a very small amount. It was just enough to help Tiger Lily pass without incident. Once again, I was reminded of the "one more thing that can go wrong" scenario. I didn't let myself dwell on the fear. I had to believe it was a good omen, that I could reinvent my career at a time when my colleagues were hanging it up. Some of them had already made it into the obituaries. That's right, screw retirement. Besides, I didn't want to die broke. I'm also determined to leave a legacy. I hope this book is one of them.

Epilogue

Every story has an end,
but in life every end is a new beginning.
—Anonymous

I like to say, what feels like the end is often the beginning. In 2007, I set out to begin a new chapter in my life. I felt a nagging urge to start writing while still running my veterinary practice in Orange County. Blogs were becoming the thing, so it was an easy platform for me to start talking. Readers of this book may be past clients or friends, or may recall my previous blog, Dog-Breath. I most enjoyed speaking my mind about controversial issues surrounding pet health care—happy to bark out warnings and challenge the status quo. But when my practice was sold a few years later, I lost my bearings to continue. No doubt the recession of 2008 – 2009 had a lot to do with the upheaval in my life, too. So, I packed my blog and stethoscope away in a storage box. I didn't need them where I was going. That rocky road trip took me on a seven-year detour. The blog, Unleashed, is my U-turn—or, as I like to say, just another beginning.

Dog-breath's mission was to answer questions—like, does my pet really need a prescription diet? No. It tackled controversial issues like vaccinations—does my pet really need all these shots? No. Its top recommendations for natural treatments, like joint supplements for arthritis, were made only after reviewing the science and studies not funded by pharmaceutical companies. It was also a call to action for other head scratchers like, is it really worth it to buy pet insurance? Yes and no. The list went on.

I was quick to defend holistically-minded pet owners on topics that sent my non-holistic colleagues to hide in closets. After the Internet got rolling, these pet owners started to arm themselves with newer information and the real battle began. I was not far behind them, asking similar questions with the mind of a true skeptic. Dismissive doctors lost clients—and rightfully so. These starchy white-coats had more opinions than any real facts or experience. Lost clients went in search of a doctor that would at least listen to them. Many had been misled by untrustworthy sources of information and misleading advertising claims. These pet owners just needed a source of reliable information to pursue other worthy, yet unconventional treatments. Some were desperately looking for any other viable option to what their vet had recommended. They all found a welcome sign on my office door up until my last working day in 2011, when Brea, California, became my rear-view mirror.

While writing this book, there have been other road signs pointing back to my roots. Most recently, I have found myself back in the kitchen. Haunting memories from a business venture that I laid to rest ten years ago started coming back into focus. It was the ghost of the Dogie Bag (Chapter Fourteen) coming back to kick my lazy butt after I finished reading a book about the canine ancestral diet. Obviously, pet food remains a hot topic being debated, especially every time new information is discovered. Being an outspoken critic of the pet food industry for most of my professional life, that debate ended for me a long time ago. Creating recipes for the Dogie Bag was my creative outlet to promote the benefits of home-cooked diets. After the big move out of O.C. lots of things changed, including my dogs' diet. I settled on a modified higher quality kibble diet, adding protein (canned fish, eggs, chicken) and veggies at mealtime. Cost and convenience became tradeoffs. I have since confessed to my dogs and have been forgiven. My dogs deserved better.

Inspired by a common-sense approach, as to what animals should be eating, health researchers are pointing us backwards to the study of ancestral diets. Before the age of modern times—more than one hundred years ago. Before someone invented the idea of selling pet food. The meat sold as "people food" is the same meat your dog should be eating. To make it easier to do, readers will find the feeding chart I created just for that reason. It's exactly what your dog wants you to read. Bone appétit.

This book and blog are dedicated to the many wonderful pet lovers I know and have yet to meet. You warm my heart and soul.

Find me "Unleashed" at PaulaTerifaj.com

About the Author

Paula Terifaj DVM graduated from the School of Veterinary Medicine at UC Davis in 1986. She claims that her veterinary career actually started in childhood when she brought home her first stray cat. She is recognized for her focus on holistic care and willingness to alert pet owners about the overuse of prescription drugs and the detriments of feeding commercial pet foods – including popular prescription diets. Paula is an animal welfare activist, public speaker and blogger.

You can find her unleashed rants and raves at:
PaulaTerifaj.com

Appendix

DR. PAULA TERIFAJ, DVM

Daily Canine Diet Guidelines Based on 10 lbs of Body Weight

The portions below are based on a 10lb dog*.
See Portion Calculator worksheet for determing portions for different body weights.

Meat .75 cup (3/4 cup)	Poultry (chicken or turkey breast; thighs without skin)
Choose 1 meat protein.	Red meat (beef, lamb, bison, etc) Boneless 90-93% lean.

Veggies .25 cup (1/4 cup)	Broccoli/brussels sprouts and other cruciferous vegetables. Pumpkin** (canned or cooked – not pie mix filling!) / zucchini and other seasonal squash.
Choose 2 or more Veggies. *Note:* Cooked or pureed veggies only (never raw). Cut all veggies into bite sized pieces. Dogs, unlike humans, cannot digest raw vegetables.	Spinach/kale and other dark leafy greens. Sweet potatoes, carrots, celery and green beans.
	**Canned or cooked pumpkin (not pie mix filling!) is recommended for its unique soluble fiber content. Helpful for both the treatment of diarrhea and constipation. The amount varies with size. A Chihuahua may only need a couple of teaspoons with each meal, whereas a Great Dane may benefit from half a cup. For dogs over 25lbs, start with 1-2 tablespoons and increase to affect.

Rotational Super Food Nutrients	.5 (1/2) Soft-cooked egg.
Rotate to include all three (eggs, organs, fish) each week. See Sample Schedule below.	4 tbsp fish. Packed in water: canned sardines, mackerel, pink salmon.
	2 tbsp poultry/red meat organs: heart, liver, gizzard.

Fruit .125 cup (1/8 cup)	Berries: blueberries / strawberry / raspberry.
Optional, but recommended. Add to meal or give as a treat. Offer only bite sized pieces or pureed.	Melons: watermelons / cantaloupe.
	Apples, pears, cucumbers and banana.
	NEVER feed grapes or raisins – reported to be toxic to dogs.

Sample Weekly Feeding Schedule

Sun	Mon	Tue	Wed	Thu	Fri	Sat
meat veggies egg	meat veggies fish	meat veggies fish	meat veggies organ meat	meat veggies organ meat	meat veggies organ meat	meat veggies egg

*10 lbs of body weight is calculated to include total daily food intake. May divide into 2 meals or feed once daily.
tbsp = tablespoon

You can download a PDF of this form at PaulaTerifaj.com

Mandatory:

Daily Calcium Supplementation for all home-cooked meals

(unless feeding raw diets that include meaty bones)

NOW™ Bone Meal *(or other human grade supplement)* OR *eggshells.*

If feeding 2 meals daily – divide the amount equally and add to each meal.

Calcium Calculator – Daily Calcium

Enter your dog's weight_____ x 25mg = _____mgs.

Example based on 40lbs:

Daily calcium needed for a 40 lb dog:

40 X 25mg = 1,000mgs (desired amount 'D')

Dried eggshells:

- Preheat the oven to 300F.
- Spread eggshells evenly on a baking sheet and bake for 5 to 7 minutes.
- Allow the eggshells to cool, then grind in a clean coffee grinder for 1 minute, or until you achieve a very fine powder with no sharp edges.
- Store at room temperature in an airtight container for up to 2 months.

- If using a **bonemeal supplement** like Now Foods (800mg of calcium per teaspoon), divide desired amount 'D' by what is available 'A'.
  (D 1000mg) ÷ (A 800mg) = 1.25 teaspoon

$$\frac{D}{A}$$ = Desired
= Available

- **Eggshells** contain roughly 2,000 mg per teaspoon (depending on size and mineral composition).(D 1000mg) ÷ (A 2000mg) = 1/2 teaspoon

- For dogs weighing 10 lb or less*:
  (D 250mg) ÷ (A 2000mg) = 0.125 or 1/8 teaspoon

*If using eggshells, use 1/8 teaspoon. Eggshell dosage does not need to be adjusted lower for dogs weighing less than 10lbs.

Strongly recommended:

Thorne™ Canine Basic Nutrients

For dogs up to 25 lbs. – one capsule daily.

Over 25 lbs. – two capsules daily. If feeding two meals – one cap per meal.

NOW™ Neptune Krill Oil capsules (or similar fatty acid profile with EPA:DHA ratios)**

One 500mg capsule 3 times/week for dogs under 50 lbs. (Give on days *not* feeding fish nutrients.)

One 1000mg capsule 3 times/week for dogs over 50 lbs. (Give on days *not* feeding fish nutrients.)

**Use only fish oil products that have been tested for purity – no mercury, PCBs or other contaminants.

Special Needs Supplement:

Nutramax Dasuquin for joints

Dose by bodyweight on label. May need to increase after 4 weeks for optimal effect.

Other

Now™ **Foods** supplements are recommended due to their high quality and affordable pricing.
The canine diet guidelines, recommended by Paula Terifaj DVM, is a modified version based on formulations in the book,
Dr. Becker's Real Food for Healthy Dogs & Cats – Fourth Edition, 2017.

You can download a PDF of this form at PaulaTerifaj.com

DR. PAULA TERIFAJ, DVM

Canine Daily Food Portion Calculator

Use this worksheet in conjuction with **Daily Canine Diet Guidelines Based on 10 lbs of Body Weight**.

> To get the proper portion for your dog, divide your dog's weight by 10, and then multiply each portion on **Daily Canine Diet Guidelines** by that number. Example: If your dog weighs 50lbs, divide by 10 to get 5. Multiple all portions by 5. Example for meat: (.75 cups) x (5) = 3.75 cups per day of meat for your 50lb dog.

Enter your dog's ideal weight: _____   ÷ 10 = _____
                                                                                                   weight factor

	weight factor		Your dog's DAILY portion
Meat: (.75 cup) x	_____	=	_____
Veggies: (.25 cup) x	_____	=	_____
Fruit: (.125 cup) x	_____	=	_____

Weekly Super Nutrients

	weight factor	weekly feeding factor	Your dog's WEEKLY portion
Egg: (.5 egg) x	_____	x2	= _____
Organ: (2 tbsp) x	_____	x3	= _____
Fish: (4 tbsp) x	_____	x2	= _____

> tbsp = tablespoon
> 1 cup = 16 tbsp
> 1/2 cup = 8 tbsp

You can download a PDF of this form at PaulaTerifaj.com

www.ingramcontent.com/pod-product-compliance
Lightning Source LLC
Chambersburg PA
CBHW021951290426
44108CB00012B/1026